How to Write and Sell Historical Fiction

How to Write and Sell

Historical Fiction

Persia Woolley

WRITER'S DIGEST BOOKS
CINCINNATI, OHIO

This hardcover edition of *How to Write and Sell Historical Fiction* features a "self-jacket" that eliminates the need for a separate dust jacket. It provides sturdy protection for your book while it saves paper, trees and energy.

Other fine Writer's Digest Books are available from your local bookstore or direct from the publisher.

01 00 99 98 97   5 4 3 2 1

Library of Congress Cataloging-in-Publication Data

Woolley, Persia.
   How to write and sell historical fiction / Persia Woolley.
     p.   cm.
   Includes index.
   ISBN 0-89879-753-5 (alk. paper)
   1. Historical fiction—Authorship. 2. Historical fiction—Marketing. I. Title.
PN3377.5.H57W66   1997
808.3'81—dc21   96-45624
                                                               CIP

Edited by Jack Heffron and Roseann S. Biederman
Production Edited by Michelle Kramer
Cover designed by Clare Finney
Interior designed by Brian Roeth

ABOUT THE AUTHOR

Persia Woolley is the author of a successful trilogy of historical novels, all published by Poseidon Press: *Child of the Northern Spring, Queen of the Summer Stars* and *Guinevere: The Legend in Autumn.* All three were selected as Book of the Month Club alternates and remain in print through Pocket Books. *Queen of the Summer Stars* was adapted as a movie for television. Woolley also has written two books for nonfiction: *Creative Survival for Single Mothers* (Celestial Arts) and *The Custody Handbook* (Summit Books). She is a frequent speaker at writer's conferences and seminars. She lives in Auburn, California.

TABLE OF CONTENTS

PREFACE

I love prefaces because they give you a chance to step out of the voice of the book and speak directly to the reader. Therefore I always encourage readers, and now specifically authors, to both read and write them. They are your opportunity to open a direct dialogue with the reader, laying out the whys and wherefores of the ensuing work, or in this case, getting a little personally reminiscent.

When I was asked to do a book on writing historical fiction I tried to pinpoint both when and why I had chosen the field myself. Though I can peg the when to a December day in 1980, the why is much more diffuse. I'm convinced we each have our own mental bulletin boards, a kind of personal refrigerator door on which random ideas and information get stuck and end up coloring the rest of our lives. And if we're lucky, sometimes we can even look back on certain moments and say, "Ah that's when the treasure map floated by; there's the fork in the road, the first hint that dreams could be spun into reality."

In my case, there are two such scraps from childhood that clearly, though inadvertently, have shaped my career.

The first took place sometime in 1945, when I accompanied my grandmother on a tiresome bus ride from Pomona to Pasadena where there was a hearing-aid office. Grandma was severely deaf, so I just rode along looking out the window at the orange groves and making up stories, which is how many children entertained themselves back in the days before TV, Walkman and Nintendo.

After a tedious stay in the rather shabby 1930s type office, it was time to go. Standing on one foot and then the other, impatient to leave, I realized my grandmother was introducing me to the nurse/receptionist behind the counter, explaining that in her spare time this woman wrote historical novels, several of which had been published.

I nodded politely, immediately forgetting the woman's name (how I wish I knew who she was now!) and then heard, very clearly, her response to my grandmother's question.

"Oh, by far the hardest part is the research. It takes such time to get it right."

Then we were out the door and the rest of the day slips into the blur of childhood. Still, that one comment lay sleeping in some cubbyhole of my mental cabinetry only to come roaring into my consciousness decades later when I decided to do a historically accurate version of the King Arthur myth from Guinevere's point of view. It was that author's admonition to "get it right" led me into months and years of research, and an entirely new career.

◆ ◆ ◆

While that chance encounter influenced my approach to historical fiction, another comment shaped the way I look at every novel, be it my own or someone else's. When I was about twelve my mother was completing a final literature course for her B.A. She had been reading one of Henry James's novels, staying up day and night, then struggling to write a paper on it. She mentioned to my grand-mother, that many scenes seemed random and extraneous, but when she read the book a second time, she discovered there wasn't a single scene which didn't contribute directly to the whole, once she understood the story.

Why that bit of literary criticism stayed in my mind, I have no idea. I wanted to be a veterinarian at that age, then later studied architecture, not creative writing, so there was no conscious desire to remember it. Nor do I have any notion which book she was referring to, and she died before I had any reason to ask her. Still and all, it's not a bad thing to keep in mind when constructing a good, solid novel.

And nowadays if someone asks me what the two most important things I strive for are when writing historical fiction, my answer is immediate—that every scene be relevant, and all the research right!

◆ ◆ ◆

No doubt you have your own specific and perhaps different criteria, just as you have your own specific reasons for wanting to write the story that made you reach for this book to begin with. You'll see as you browse this volume that I'll encouraging you to find your own voice, choose your own sequences, tell your own tales. Like Anais Nin, I feel we need more voices, not fewer, and if this work helps others to put their story on paper, I'll be satisfied.

In the following chapters we'll look at different kinds of histori-cals, the possibilities and limitations of research, how to plot and develop characters, integrate history with your own fictional people, choose points of view, edit, find an agent and—it should only-happen—cope with publishers, critics and Hollywood. After all, if you're going to dream, go ahead and dream big. Just remember that old saying: "Why wish for a loaf of bread when you can wish for the country store?"

There are a number of professionals who helped make this book possible and deserve many thanks; first off, Parke Godwin, my neighbor and fellow novelist who's shared many hours of his experiences with me, and Merrilee Heifetz, who has taught me what a jewel a good agent is, and revived my faith in the breed. Thanks also to Gail Golomb and Grant Gibbs of Four Geez Press, who have been unstinting in help, support and contacts, and the many librarians at the Auburn Placer Library who have helped me check out innumerable bits of literary history, anecdotes and spellings.

Finally, of course, to my editors Jack Heffron and Roseann Biederman whose encouragement and good eye have kept me from straying too far from the point, and Michelle Kramer whose good auspices saw the book into production.

In an effort to cope with the English language's lack of a pronoun for an individual that is not gender specific, we have arbitrarily alternated between "he" and "she." The choice is sometimes awkward, but is used specifically so as not to slight either gender.

The major purpose of this work has been to pass on all the hints, helps and forewarnings I could think of, and make available all the information I wish I'd had, but didn't, when I started out. May it make your path a little easier, and just as much fun.

Persia Woolley

July 14, 1996
Auburn, CA.

PART ONE

In the Beginning

CHAPTER ONE

What Are We Talking About Here?

S o you want to write historical fiction. You've got this wonderful idea floating around in your head, and while you believe in it, you're not sure how to put it down on paper, where to start your research, when to begin writing, how to wrap it up and what happens after you've told your tale.

Or maybe you're worried about how much time and money your research will take. Or if anyone else will be interested. Or whether it's worth investing a portion of your life to find out.

Well, don't feel bad. Every one of the authors you enjoy reading was originally in your situation. Once upon a time we were all hopeful novelists, holding down regular jobs and scribbling away on "the book" at night and on weekends. (No matter how many you've done, the current project is always "the book," as though no others have ever existed.) Or we were journalists who secretly yearned to be doing the necessary research and making the switch to fiction. Or professors aching to turn the acquired knowledge of an academic career into a popular best-seller so we'd never have to cope with college politics again. Ask any historical author and you'll find someone who stood at the same juncture you're at now and wished there was a book on how to make the switch.

Unfortunately, no book can provide you with the inner determination (or desperation) it takes to make the switch—that has to come from you. But this book can fill in some of the blanks and give you as much in the way of encouragement and helpful hints as possible.

Everyone pays his dues in this business—usually in learning just what the publishing world is all about—and all writers develop "tricks of the trade" both for constructing and telling our stories and for handling the professionals who print our work. Over the years I've listened to a lot of writers sharing their experiences and expertise, and I've included as much of that as possible in this tome. While there are prima donnas in every art, we all generally look back on our own beginnings with bemusement and shock at how innocent we were and are willing to give a mental hand to others who are starting out.

Probably the most important factor you need to consider right from the beginning is that writing historical fiction is far more than a career: It generally becomes a way of life. Neither as remunerative as brain surgery, nor as taxing as being a carpenter, it isn't as organized as punching a clock at a factory or as secure as being a garbage collector. People who make their livings in those fields know when, where and how their checks will arrive. And usually they can count on what size those checks will be.

Most novelists can't rely on any of these things, and if you're a beginner, you could get anywhere from $2,500 to $250,000 for your first novel, depending on timing, the needs of the market, your agent and a lot of plain old luck—*if* it gets published, that is.

So if it's that unreliable, why does anyone want to be a novelist, much less a writer of *historical* fiction?

Most of us will tell you it's because writing is the most exciting and pleasurable way there is to make a living, and it has a hundred extra perks that make up for the lack of money. Not only are you your own boss keeping your own hours, with the constant challenge of research or writing filling every day, there's also the outside chance you might hit it big. And while I don't advocate that as anything to count on, the fact remains, I'd still be a middle-aged divorcée working in an office with no future if I hadn't decided to write my first novel. When the risk pays off, it's worthwhile.

Nor am I the only one who feels this way—in any group of twenty people picked at random, at least two of them will tell you they *want* to write a novel, or possibly have already started. Not all want to do historicals, of course, but the desire to capture an event in words and entertain others at the same time is so basic, it could easily be called the third oldest profession, after warmongering and prostitution.

FAMILY FABLES

The first stories no doubt started as tribal history. People gathered around the fire, telling what their ancestors did or didn't do.

Sometimes the unexpected was explained as divine intervention, so you might say history and religion had a twin conception.

Usually tales were based on the activities of the specific family or tribe and were told with characters so memorable and deeds so daring, the story was handed on to the next generation.

(Preliterate societies, which have not yet begun writing things down, have wonderfully vivid legends for precisely this reason. Since the audience can't look up the story in a book later, the storyteller has to make it as dramatic and colorful as possible so it will stick in everyone's memory. Keep this in mind if you have a bard or troubadour in your work. Let him use dramatic language, grand gestures, flamboyant voice and mime, all the time checking to make sure he hasn't lost his audience. It will heighten both the impact of the story your reader is following and the ambiance of the world you're creating.)

As time went on, these tales evolved because each generation of storytellers added to their patina by embellishing, moralizing and acting out what should have taken place, even if it hadn't. The next thing you know, you've got historical fiction; stories that might have been—or ought to be—true but somehow lack the "proof" that is thought to add veracity to straight history.

There are people who claim that history is just fiction written by the winners, and there may be something to that. Certainly it usually has a particular bias. But now, at the turn of the twenty-first century, historical fiction has a strong appeal and steady market among booksellers, so let's get down to definitions and specifics so that you can get on with your writing and have your book take its place on their shelves.

WHAT IS HISTORICAL FICTION?

One of the first things I did on getting this assignment was ask people who their favorite historical novelists were. Surprisingly, Jane Austen's name came up more than once. Austen was indeed a fine writer, and deservedly popular even today. But she wrote about the people and society of her own contemporary world, and though that makes it "historical" to us, does that mean she qualifies as a historical novelist? Wasn't she really more of an early Tom Wolfe than a James Michener?

The same holds true for Emily Brontë, author of *Wuthering Heights,* and Gustave Flaubert, whose *Madame Bovary* so outraged his contemporary Frenchmen, both he and his book were put on trial for the deeds of the (very fictional) heroine—probably a first in the history of jurisprudence.

All of these authors and works were dealing with their own societies, yet many people think of them as historical because they reflect an era long gone. Which brings up the question of how to define historical fiction.

For the sake of this work, let's define historical fiction as set in a time other than that of the reader, with characters that react in some degree to the historical events of their eras. It may or may not reflect the actual life experiences of the author, but it interests readers in part because it is different from their present culture.

(It's both easier and chancier to do contemporary books; since both author and reader have lived through the same time frame, the audience is more knowledgeable and possibly more critical of your take on things. And while you can refer to something as all-pervasive as a Big Mac and strike a familiar chord with your readers, you may also date the work considerably as far as future audiences are concerned.)

Sometimes a historical novel is located in a foreign country. Yet even if you're writing about your own backyard, the difference in time will mean that the social mores and patterns will be different. In the 1960s someone put out a booklet from the 1800s that cautioned young men, "Never give a lady a restive horse." While that's hardly part of the etiquette of courtship nowadays, it was applicable for any swain in any town in the United States at the time it was originally written and illustrates how exotic our own past can seem from even a few decades distance.

By defining historical fiction in terms of the reader's frame of reference, we have enough latitude to look at works as diverse as Gore Vidal's *Lincoln* and Mary Renault's *The King Must Die*; Margaret Mitchell's *Gone With the Wind* and Boris Pasternak's *Doctor Zhivago*; Parke Godwin's *Sherwood* and my own Guinevere trilogy, *Child of the Northern Spring, Queen of the Summer Stars* and *Guinevere: the Legend in Autumn.*

Of these, Pasternak's is the only novel set in his own lifetime—all the rest deal with historical settings anywhere from decades to millennia before their authors were born. While I haven't been able to determine how much of *Doctor Zhivago* was drawn from Pasternak's own experience during the Russian Revolution, the work is such a classic example of its kind, whether it's autobiographical or not is irrelevant.

THE LITERATE BARDS

So who writes historical novels? Men and women, young and old, you name it and there will be a representative among the authors. Lew Wallace was a military officer in both the Mexican-American and the Civil Wars who reached the rank of major general, served as Governor of New Mexico and became a diplomat to Turkey. In between he authored *Ben Hur*, which was incredibly popular as a book and a play during the late 1800s, and as a movie continues to delight audiences with a fine mixture of adventure and history.

In Britain the charming, white-haired widow of an English parson writes about ancient Egypt and Nefertiti. In South Africa a husky spinster became a specialist in classical Greece as she researched her novels set in that era. Here in the States a major bestselling writer of suspense turned his hand to medieval cathedral building, and a science fiction/fantasy author has written several superb books dealing with gritty, nonfantasy Saxon history.

Who reads historical fiction? Again the range is enormous. James Michener is world famous for his books, which are read by both men and women, adult and youngster. Colleen McCullough's Australian saga, *The Thorn Birds*, is another example of work that achieved a worldwide audience and was enjoyed by people in all walks of life. And her Roman books, which we'll discuss later, are well received by scholars as well as fans of all ages.

I sometimes wonder why historicals are so popular. What, aside from the obvious storytelling abilities of the aforementioned authors, attracts readers by the thousands?

It seems to be a combination of education and curiosity. Many people say they've learned more about a particular era or event through good historical fiction than any other means. Certainly if the storyteller is gifted, she can bring that period of time to life in a way few academic scholars can.

One of my stepdaughters hated history in school but would listen, enthralled, while I outlined the course of the Tudor reign in England. "Well," she announced, "you make it sound like family gossip, not boring history." Probably the fact that I think of every leader in the world as just another human being underneath the pomp or pretense is why I could make it interesting to her and what's led me to concentrate on historicals. Not only does this approach humanize past events, historicals provide room for speculation as to why things happened the way they did.

Another reason for the appeal of historical fiction may lie in the fact that the present-day world is full of high-tech language and tools and a constantly increasing level of man-made stress. By comparison, there's something reassuring about picking up a book in which the biggest calamities are natural disasters and your enemy can't threaten to wipe you out by pushing a distant button, but has to face you eye to eye.

Then, too, historical novels usually encourage a broader range of thought than the action-packed violence of contemporary movies and television. You have a chance to savor and absorb the various characters, think about the philosophies espoused, examine the world more slowly instead of being overwhelmed by one adrenaline rush after another. Gut reaction is all very fine, but not on every page. Also, earlier eras are safe in that you know the world didn't come to an end and you can tap into a kind of nostalgia and security because of it.

Probably all of these things contribute to why people read such works. Certainly they are a major part of why some of us spend our lives writing them.

WHY *THAT* BOOK?

What makes a particular author choose to write a specific book? There tend to be four basic sources of inspiration, and each produces a different kind of book.

The first is when the writer has a particular fondness for or knowledge of a special era, such as Boris Pasternak, whose *Doctor Zhivago* gave the world an inside view of how the Russian Revolution affected the average citizen. This is a fine example of a novel that is history driven, and it will be examined more fully in the next chapter.

Then there's the author who's hounded by a specific character or concept that keeps demanding to be put down on paper. In my case it was a realistic Guinevere, a whole and honest person who wouldn't let me rest. The usual presentation of Arthur's queen as a kind of beautiful twit whose only function was to be a love object seemed terribly two-dimensional, so I decided to redress that with a more historically probable portrayal. That was the mandate in my mind, though I had no idea when she would have actually lived. If it turned out she and Arthur had originated in medieval times, I would have put them there instead of at the beginning of Britain's Dark Ages, because it was the character rather than the era that attracted me.

Some authors are hooked on a particular event. Parke Godwin became fascinated with the dynamics in England following its conquest by William of Normandy. Here was a fully functioning, somewhat insular nation of sturdy farmers suddenly under the yoke of the far more sophisticated but equally narrow-minded Europeans; naturally there would have been fireworks. (The play and movie *Becket* explores that relationship in the twelfth century when it had been going on for a number of decades. How much more explosive it must have been in 1070, when William's reign was new and even more resented!)

Godwin proposed a book about the Saxon/Norman conquest and was turned down—no major historical characters to hang a title on, and the publishers weren't interested in everyday people. They were interested, however, in a retelling of the Robin Hood myth because Kevin Costner was making a film about that figure, and they wanted a book to come out that same summer and ride along on the interest the movie created. So could Godwin please come up with something about those men in green tights?

Godwin not only could but did. As with King Arthur, there is no proof of the historical reality of Robin Hood, but in legend he was a minor aristocrat who became an outlaw rather than go along with a corrupt overlord. Tradition (mostly established by another historical novelist, Sir Walter Scott in his work *Ivanhoe*) has placed Robin Hood in the late 1100s, during the reign of Richard the Lion-Heart. It was but a small step for Godwin to shift Robin back to the time immediately after William's conquest, and voila, the same dynamics apply but with much more drama and accuracy. The results were *Sherwood* and *Robin and the King*, both of which are excellent reads.

For once you had an author who was able to satisfy the itch to write about a certain event and a publisher who got the subject he felt was more commercially viable, so everyone benefited.

The fourth reason for writing a particular historical novel was mentioned by Colleen McCullough in regard to her Roman books (*The First Man of Rome, The Grass Crown, Fortune's Favorite* and

Caesar's Women): No one else had explored the subject in depth. Imperial Rome, yes. Classical Greece, yes. The late Republic, no. So she staked out her subject and went after it.

McCullough is a writer's writer who likes to write different things because they are challenging, interesting or haven't been done before. Thus she classifies her first book, *Tim*, as a love story, *The Thorn Birds* as a gothic romance, *Credo for the Third Millennia* as a futuristic work and the Roman books as true historicals.

Most authors aren't given that kind of latitude, as publishers want to stick with what they know can sell. After the amazing success of *The Thorn Birds*—for years it was the biggest seller since *Gone With the Wind*—McCullough's publisher wanted her to go on producing gothic romances. Fortunately for her readers, the money generated by *The Thorn Birds* meant she could do pretty much what she wanted, and the Roman books were the result.

WHAT DOES IT TAKE TO BECOME A HISTORICAL NOVELIST?

Most importantly, you need to be a storyteller first, a historian second. While a good grasp of your era is essential both to plot and writing, if you haven't mastered the art of storytelling, you're not going to get very far. As an old-time actor used to say, "People care about what happens to people, so keep the characters downstage of the scenery."

There is a caution in that as well. If history is your first love, you'd be best advised to stick with nonfiction. From personal experience, I know how easy it is to get swept up in the intricacies of how or why a historical event took place, but if it interferes with the flow of your fictional story, no one will buy it.

If you're a first-time novelist, you'll need to write the entire manuscript from beginning to end on your own time, without a contract agreement or an advance. There's good reason for this: Even journalists who do a good job with nonfiction may not be able to sustain the reader's interest in fictional characters. It takes a particular knack to have your characters act out their story, and in this case the proof of the pudding is, truly, in the result. So even if you've a ton of nonfiction credits to your name, both agents and publishers are going to want to see a completed work before investing their time and money in your novel.

Which means you'll need to do your initial research, plotting, writing and editing on your own, squeezing the time in between other commitments and hoping you're on the right track.

If it's any consolation, all first-time novelists go through this process. It's called "writing on spec," that is, you're gambling that the finished product will be salable. The difference for a historical novelist is the amount of time and money that goes into research and the necessity of integrating that research into your story.

SO WHAT DO YOU GET IN RETURN?

Most all books require *some* research, if only to confirm things that we ourselves lived through but have gotten hazy on, such as the month the Beatles first appeared on the Ed Sullivan show or the year the Ford Mustang was introduced. Then, too, contemporary novelists frequently choose themes that broaden their own horizons and they end up learning about the care and feeding of polo ponies or the running of a soup kitchen in the inner city, depending on which end of the financial spectrum they're writing about.

Historical fiction that is set in both a different era and a different locale requires even more research. And while the level of both time and money committed to it will vary with each author, many historical novelists get so deeply involved in the history and culture they're writing about, they become experts in the field.

Mary Renault, the English woman who chose to live in South Africa, accumulated what was undoubtedly the best and most comprehensive library on classical Greece to be found south of the equator. Her correspondence with specialists all over the world must be fascinating and certainly kept her from feeling isolated in her distant home.

Colleen McCullough has done the same with books from, about and by the Romans of the Republic, and she lives on an island in the South Pacific. And to this day I am occasionally contacted to verify or teach things about Dark Ages Britain because the eleven years of research I put into my Guinevere trilogy made me one of the most widely read people on the era.

Then, too, all that research is not only mentally challenging and enjoyable, it can include all sorts of tax-deductible trips to the locations of your book. I am presently completing a large regional historical entitled *Sierra*, which has taken up six years of my life and allowed me to cruise both lake and river on paddle wheel steamers, ride in Wells Fargo stages and camp along the Pony

Express route over the Sierra Nevada mountains, all as part of my research. And for a proposed book on the Trojan War, I'll be contacting various archaeologists so a visit to the actual ruins may be possible. Certainly the five trips I made to Britain for Guinevere were a delight, even though they were accomplished under strong financial and time constraints.

Most of us find that the mental challenge of learning about new eras keeps us pliant and flexible mentally, which is always nice. When dealing with older times, you need to consider a vast array of subjects that were different in those days. You may find yourself consulting herbal medicine books and practitioners, since the drugs we rely on today are almost all synthetic and quite new to mankind's pharmacopiea. Or learning the best kind of wagon for taking on the Emigrant Trail (a lightweight one that can be used as a farm wagon once you get where you're going—Conestogas, while popular in folk legend, were too big and unwieldy to make it over the mountains). Or perhaps you'll need to practice carding fleece, identifying opium bottles or estimating where the Romans built practice camps in Britain. And investigating every aspect of a different era or locale gives you plenty of opportunity to meet new people who already know what you're asking about, which is a further plus.

Clearly, if you are of a curious bent it's a lifestyle that offers endless possibilities. As my children are fond of saying, it also keeps me off the streets. And as I like to point out, it has the potential of paying big dividends—not the promise, but the potential. For a major sale is, after all, the hope and dream of all writers. It may not be the only motivation, but it's certainly nice when it happens.

CHAPTER TWO

How Much Fact, How Much Fiction?

arke Godwin turned a nice phrase when he said the historical novelist is one who synthesizes fact and fiction. He was speaking particularly about those of us who take a legend and, after tracing it back to its probable origins, set out to retell it in real, historical terms. But the same definition can just as easily apply to a historical novel that is not based on a previous legend, but made up from and for the author's own experience.

Godwin also speaks of how a writer is constantly making choices—what tense, whose point of view, which sequence, how long or abbreviated and so forth. Fortunately for most of us, it's an unconscious process, part of the storytelling knack, and happens whether we think about it or not.

Still, there are some decisions that have to be made early on, particularly if you hope to introduce your finished product to agents and publishers. They're going to ask you what your book is, as well as what it is about, and you'll do well to have a good, clear handle on the answer.

LARGE OR SMALL, PERIOD PIECE OR HISTORICAL

These are the most basic choices of all: Are you aiming to craft a small gem such as Conrad Richter's *Sea of Grass* or a huge epic along the lines of Tolstoy's *War and Peace?*

They are two entirely different art forms: Tolstoy's epic traces the interweaving and development of various characters in several families all reacting to war, peace and each other, and is a massive and involving masterpiece; whereas Richter's very slim volume focuses entirely on the husband's compulsive desire to keep settlers out of what he sees as his rightful domain. This ruins both his own humanity and his relationships with wife, friend and son, which leads to a cross-generational tragedy. Sound dull? That's the challenge of a short novel—even in description or criticism, it's a lot easier to wax eloquent about a big convoluted work than it is to capture the lean, jewel-like quality of a classic such as *Sea of Grass*.

Both forms are equally viable, and as with everything else, there are pros and cons to each approach. Although a small book doesn't give you the space to develop matters in depth, neither can you go too far astray, so it probably equals out. A large book, on the other hand, hangs around your life forever, becomes part of your family, your dreams, even your dinner-table conversation: Instead of "What did you do at the office today, dear?" it's "Did your heroine escape from the bear trap, dear?"

Joking aside, there is something both substantive and satisfying about guiding your characters through a saga over a period of time, in part because you come to know them so well, though how Tolstoy managed to keep track of the entire cast of *War and Peace*, I'll never understand.

Only you, as the author, can know how big your project should be, either in time dedicated to it or in the size of the finished work. And even that can change as the book progresses. I assumed that my Guinevere would be one volume when I began my research, but long before I actually started writing, it was clear that what I had was, by nature, a trilogy. Just remember Chopin's admonition to George Sand when she complained about the brevity of a particular piece: Any creative work should be only as long as its content dictates. That's advice you might want to recall from time to time.

Another aspect to consider is how big a role history itself plays in your story. At a writers conference recently, one of the romance authors mentioned that she had written three "period pieces"— novels set in a specific time frame but not impacted by specific historical events—and one "historical novel" wherein both people and events of the real world were involved with her story.

It's a good differentiation to make. Period pieces require less knowledge of the specific events of your era (and therefore possibly less research), though they may lack a sense of tie-in with the rest of the world, as if the characters lived in a vacuum. I'm not sure that one is better or more popular than the other, but they are options to keep in mind when trying to describe your book to an agent or publisher.

Obviously historical fiction comes in all sizes and forms and ranges from pure history to pure fiction with just a background smattering and occasional bold stroke of history interjected. A look at the best will give you some idea of what makes for a good read and provide you with a list of books to look for if you haven't discovered them on your own.

HISTORY IN NOVEL FORM: *THE KILLER ANGELS*

This Pulitzer Prize-winning reconstruction of the four days of Gettysburg by William Shaara is both totally grounded in research and soaring in its portrayal of the different men involved in one of the turning points of our nation's history.

In his "Note to the Reader," Shaara mentions that Stephen Crane said he wrote *The Red Badge of Courage* because reading cold history was not enough; he wanted to know what it was like to *be* there, and in order to live it, he had to write it.

That's a wonderful explanation of why we write historicals, and Shaara's work comes as close as any I've found to actually fulfilling that promise to the reader.

Yet, even though Shaara's work is about as authentic as one can get—in his research he went back to primary sources, the actual diaries, letters and words of the men involved—he also gets inside the characters' heads to create the ambiance, tension, drama and excitement that we associate more with fiction than with history.

Not many writers of any generation can pull it off as well as he has, and every hopeful historical novelist would do well to read this book and study it for clarity, structure and transparent writing where the words seem to melt away and the reader experience the story rather than the act of reading.

MYTH AS HISTORY—THE EUHEMERIST

At the other end of the spectrum is the story (or legend) that's treated as history. I have a friend who points out that if the western mind can't measure a thing, it treats it as if it didn't exist. One of his favorite examples is the fact that there must be tides in a teacup, we just deny their existence because they aren't easy to measure.

Legends and folktales used to fit into that category too, as long as they couldn't be specifically verified. For centuries people shrugged them off as wishful thinking, and it was only when Henry Schliemann actually located the fabled city of Troy by following the route described in Homer that historians began to wonder if there might be something behind these legends after all.

It wasn't long before enterprising novelists and playwrights began mining legends, looking for the real people living in real time whose actions could have sown the seeds of what became fantastic tales. Henry Treece was one such author, working in the 1950s and providing extremely gritty retellings of both Greek and European myths in real terms.

I was bemused to find there is a specific term for such writers. They're called euhemerists, which means, according to the dictionary, "people who see myths as traditional accounts of historical persons and events."

Euhemerists study not only the legends that attract them and the historical eras when they began, but also their growth as a folktales over the centuries. Generally this is to weed out those things that are later additions, but while I was working on the Guinevere books, I ran across something that played right into the development of my characters. Until the French troubadours got hold of the story in the twelfth century, King Arthur's primary warrior and champion was his nephew, Gawain. Indeed, in the earliest tales, which date roughly from seventh to tenth century, Gawain was the exemplary gentleman, courtly with the ladies, brave, a tenacious fighter and loyal to his friends.

But with the introduction of Lancelot (a distinctly French addition), Gawain's prestige began to slip and he was being portrayed in the newer stories as less gallant in comparison to the continental newcomer. Pretty soon he became downright boorish, contentious and untrustworthy, seducing his friend's fiancée and turning violently against Lancelot, finally goading Arthur into declaring war on the Frenchman after Lance saved the queen's life.

In looking at the literary development, it struck me that it paralleled the sort of sibling rivalry that develops when you introduce a new and highly visible personality into a family . . . so I used that same dynamic within my fictional character, thereby getting a chance to show Gawain's better side early on and his development into a jealous and vindictive competitor for Arthur's love and trust as the books went on.

Euhemerists also constantly mine their legends for hints, tips, clues and hooks on which to hang some real explanation of what is seen as magical or otherworldly in mythic form. One of the foremost among such writers is Mary Renault, whose Theseus novels, *The King Must Die* and *The Bull From the Sea*, have become classics in their own right.

In the legend, Theseus rids the land of numerous monsters, sometimes with weapons, sometimes just by his own prowess; he is said to have developed the art of Greek wrestling. His father, the king of Athens, has left behind not only an unwed mother, but also a pair of sandals and a sword, hidden under a rock, with instructions for his son (Theseus) to bring them to Athens when he is strong enough to lift the rock, that is, when he's a full-grown adult, old enough and mature enough to take his father's place.

With a stroke of creative brilliance, Renault makes her Theseus a small lad who has to learn wrestling early on just to hold his own among his peers. And having discovered the importance of leverage, he moves the rock out of the way much sooner than his father had expected, arriving in Athens while still young enough to be sent to Crete as one of the sacrificial youths Athens was forced to supply the Minoans on a regular basis.

The decision to make Theseus small and clever enough to become adept at wrestling explains his phenomenal success in physical battles as well, and he becomes a hero we in the twentieth century can identify with—a man who takes hold of his own life's challenges and overcomes the odds by ingenuity, not by relying on the whim of some god to come to his aid.

In *The King Must Die* Renault also introduces two ancient concepts that had only been rediscovered in the twentieth century: the idea of the royal sacrifice—that the king must be willing to give up his life for his people if necessary—and the newly excavated murals in Knossos's palace on Crete, which show youths performing acrobatic feats between the horns and over the back of a charging bull. It was the sight of these vital and vibrant pictures that gave Renault the inspiration to connect Theseus with these "bull-dancers" and started her on the path of writing the books.

Sometimes it happens that there are several versions of the same myth. Theseus, for instance, is said to be the son of the sea-god Poseidon as well as the traveling king of Athens, which would indicate that there were originally two different stories. It was not uncommon for heroes to be given divine fathers—look at all those half-god, half-human children Zeus left lying around—once their deeds of daring and popular appeal are clearly established.

Even Merlin was said to have un-human origins, a fact that Mary Stewart plays on with great results in the first of her Merlin trilogy, *The Crystal Cave*. What better way to conceal the identity of a politically unacceptable lover than by claiming it was a spirit, god or demon who got you pregnant?

Sometimes opposing versions of a legend can be used to add tension within the euhemerist's work. There is a branch of the Arthurian myth that suggests Guinevere was complicit in her own kidnapping and rape, thereby indicating she was a devious, untrustworthy and disloyal wife to Arthur.

Since I had made her abductor a cousin she had known and disliked for years (he is also a real historical tyrant from that era), it seemed natural that she would try to stall for time when he comes to see her the first time. So I have her playing a famous game of chess with him, trying to throw him off base while the serving woman is bringing them food, etc. The servant is, clearly, in the employee of Morgan le Fey, who has her own reasons for hating Gwen. Once Gwen is rescued and returned to Arthur, rumors that she was not an unwilling partner to her cousin begin to circulate, put forth by Morgan's camp. The reader knows it isn't true, but I was able to use this other version to heighten the tension between Arthur and Gwen when she returns to him and to show that Morgan will use any means to destroy Gwen in the eyes of Arthur and the world.

These are just a few examples of what the euhemerist does and how, if you want to retell a mythical story, you need to start with the given plot and work backward, looking for realistic explanations and honest motivations to elevate the fairy tale to truly epic levels of human achievement.

◆ ◆ ◆

Sometimes you'll run across comments about a specific book being character driven or plot driven. Although these terms are fairly self-explanatory, someone recently said that literature was usually the slower character-driven work, while popular entertainment (such as the work of Tom Clancy) relies heavily on the faster, plot-driven story.

Oddly enough, it seems to be the reverse in historical fiction. The novel with a history-driven plot requires more background, buildup and understanding, whereas the character-driven piece can whiz by at whatever pace the author is able to maintain. There are two classic examples, each of which deal with civil war, anarchy and unattainable love, yet even though they are both classics, they are about as different as one can imagine.

HISTORY DRIVEN: *DOCTOR ZHIVAGO*

In Boris Pasternak's *Doctor Zhivago*, history is the major impetus of the plot; if you read the book straight through, then look back on it as a whole, you'll find that most of the characters are shaped by events over which they have no control. Far more importantly, each is symbolic of a particular strand in the national makeup, so although they are specific individuals, they are also icons of a sort, which gives the book a great deal of its power.

Zhivago represents the Russian people. His antecedents are vague, and his mother dies early; we first meet him as a young boy watching her coffin being buried under wide gray skies out on the edge of nowhere. It is a haunting scene that gives a kind of rootless, almost nomadic quality to his soul—as though he might be anyone, anywhere—as well as reflecting the tremendous power of the land on the Russian heart and soul.

He is taken in by a moderately well-off family of distant relatives who make sure he is not only educated, but engaged to their daughter as well. As a person he is genuinely concerned about others, curious about the world, but more or less uncritical in his acceptance of life. A thoughtful man, he can articulate his emotions, but rarely attempts to take hold of his destiny and change things.

His fiancée is sent away to be educated in France (as was the custom among the wealthier people), so she carries the veneer of western culture, which was important to the upper middle class. But it is Lara, a half-French working-class girl (who is seduced early on and kept by her mother's lover, an attorney of high money and low character) who proves to be Zhivago's great love.

These two young women reflect Russia's own love-hate relationship with France, from whom she learned much but to whom nationals claimed she had prostituted herself.

Lara comes to represent Mother Russia; at one point Zhivago actually calls her that. Earthy, sturdy, beautiful in a vital, unconscious way, she is his lodestar, his beacon, the thing that keeps him going when the chaos of civil war has torn everyone's world apart.

But Lara loves and marries a young revolutionary, much as the Russian people flocked to and espoused the revolution in 1917. Eventually this husband deserts her for the Cause and by the end of the book he's become a dehumanized fanatic whose very presence is a threat to her safety—a nice tidy bit of symbolism. Though they meet early on, there is no romance between Lara and Zhivago, both because of their different classes and the fact that she is otherwise occupied, first with the lawyer, then with the revolutionary. Only when they work together as medics on the German front during World War I do she and the doctor begin to fall in love.

The middle part of the book deals largely with the struggle to survive the Bolshevik Revolution and disintegration of life as lack of food and fuel in the city threatens everyone's survival. Even after Zhivago takes his family back to the land, there are the difficulties of establishing some sort of life and sustenance, as well as the surprising discovery that Lara lives in a nearby village. It is here that she and the doctor consummate their love in an adulterous affair.

Zhivago's conscience is as much at war in him as are the Red and White partisans that roam across the countryside, alternately capturing or losing different enclaves. One of these gangs takes the doctor prisoner, putting him to use among their wounded, and it is hundreds—maybe thousands—of days and miles before he is able to escape and begin walking endlessly back to wife and children.

More dead than alive, he staggers into the village, only to find that his family has fled Russia. For a little while he and Lara share an intensely romantic idyl in spite of the famine and freezing winter around them, until the villainous lawyer arrives with a warning that she is in danger of arrest and execution because of her husband's activities. Zhivago refuses to go but sends her away with brave promises that he will follow shortly, though they never meet again. Later the reader discovers Lara was willing to leave him only because she was carrying his child.

The book ends on the same almost bleak note on which it began, with Zhivago spending a last decade back in Moscow, living and working in a state of seedy decline, taken in by a family he's known before and producing several progeny by their daughter who reveres him deeply. Only when he dies does Lara come forward for the funeral, happening into the house in search of old friends and finding instead the body of her lover. There is a deeply touching scene where she bids farewell to Zhivago in the coffin and agrees to help his half brother organize his notes and poems into a book. But before long she disappears; possibly, it is hinted, she's arrested and sent to die in one of Stalin's camps.

In the epilogue we meet their daughter who is as rootless and confused as the generation that followed the Revolution. A waif who thinks herself an orphan, she does not know she is the child of Zhivago and Lara, whose love has become famous through the Zhivago poems. The author flat out says that one sometimes finds the children of idealists and great lovers are made of much drosser stuff, and the book ends on a kind of distant, bittersweet nostalgia for the lovers from the past.

Pasternak was awarded the Nobel Prize for *Doctor Zhivago*, not only because of its fine writing (unfortunately the English translation doesn't do the poet's prose justice) but also because it records a time of intense national crisis long hidden behind the communist curtain of silence. Certainly it achieves a splendid balance between fictional characters that you care about and their power as icons of Russia's recent history.

Anyone looking for a lush, romantic saga akin to *Gone With the Wind* will find this book a disappointment. But for those interested in the kind of tapestry that historical novels can provide, it is a breathtaking work that offers believable characters laughing, loving and fighting desperately in a world gone mad.

CHARACTER DRIVEN: *GONE WITH THE WIND*

By contrast, Margaret Mitchell's *Gone With the Wind* is character driven all the way, with the willful and self-centered Scarlett O'Hara dominating the entire book. The palette of characterization, point of view and depth of thought is flamboyant and shallow compared to *Doctor Zhivago*.

There is plenty of history in the background, what with the American Civil War and Reconstruction (throwing your characters' world into havoc always promises lots of drama and tension), and Mitchell's people also reflect different segments of society, but since the point of view is almost always Scarlett's, and her one interest is herself and Ashley, the historical aspects of the story are almost incidental.

Thus, though it starts the day before Fort Sumter is fired on and the Civil War begins, the first few chapters focus entirely on Scarlett's background and personality, the establishing of southern attitudes and the famous barbecue at Twelve Oaks. Scarlett is determined to surround herself with as many men as she can in order to make Ashley jealous, and even the news of the coming hostilities doesn't phase her until she realizes that Ashley will be going away— possibly to get killed—and he intends to marry Melanie Hamilton before leaving. Frantic with anger, shock and heartbreak, she throws herself into a totally unsuitable marriage with Melanie's brother after having an infuriating confrontation with the scoundrel Rhett Butler.

As you can see, even though history is making its demands on the lives of the characters, the author's attention and point of view remain focused on the tempestuous Scarlett, who flat out says she doesn't give a fig about the war. Her reactions are totally subjective and self-serving, and historical events are kept firmly in the background while the reader becomes intensely involved with Scarlett's personality.

Mitchell makes the choice not to bring historical figures on stage, though Sherman and Johnston are mentioned several times. Even Sherman's march to the sea is personalized in the encounter between Scarlett and an anonymous Union soldier who is intent on stealing her mother's earrings. Mitchell makes it a contest between Scarlett and the specific threat, so instead of reflecting the conflict between North and South, it serves mainly to establish that Scarlett will stop at nothing to protect Tara and her way of life.

There is little that is introspective in Scarlett—no probing of philosophical depths, no questioning anything other than how to get what she wants. She goes from being a spoiled vixen to a greedy vamp, apparently without ethics or honor, and as Mitchell said several times in interviews, it is Melanie who is the heroine, not Scarlett. Yet the book—and characters—continue to captivate us.

One reason for this is that Mitchell constructs an entire world for us through her choice of scenes which convey both the circumstances and lifestyles of her people. Early on Scarlett's mother, Ellen, is shown to be the gracious lady, tending to the needs of slave and poorer neighbors when they are sick or birthing. Thus we see landed gentry following the philosophy of *noblesse oblige*: the various classes living in close proximity, with the white-trash Slatterys on the edge of the O'Hara's property, Tara, and the wealthy, aristocratic Wilkes family at Twelve Oaks just beyond. It is also established, more as a color than an actual theme, that there is minimal fuss over childbirth, with no thought of calling in a doctor or heading for the hospital.

That's a lot of information to convey so quickly, and Mitchell manages to do it with remarkable ease.

There are many other scenes that are rich in texture and information as well as being memorable because of the characters. Who can forget Scarlett's determination and inventiveness in using her mother's green velvet drapes to make a dress in which to seduce Rhett when Tara is in danger of being sold for taxes? Or, of course, her classically childish response of "I'll think about it tomorrow," when confronted with anything that is vaguely uncomfortable.

Mitchell's original draft involved a good deal more in the way of historical material, but she was asked to take it out because it was felt it would slow down the story for the reader. She did so (though not without making several tart comments), and certainly the pace of the saga rarely sags.

EDUCATION OR ENTERTAINMENT: *THE FIRST MAN IN ROME*

The problem of historical material vs. fictitious action is one that crops up constantly. Part of it is, I suspect, cultural: Readers who did not grow up with slam-bang entertainment, motormouthed radio announcers and an attention span of less than three minutes seem to prefer books that explore the background and dynamics of a situation. They are among those who continue to buy and read James Michener, for instance. Many other readers, used to channel surfing, sound bites and instant gratification, have no interest in exploring a matter in greater depth and demand a rapid pace that covers lots of ground.

This can result in the classic conflict between the commercially oriented agent or publisher who says, "Get rid of the history so we can sell more books," and the author who cries, "How can I show what's affecting them if I take it all out?"

Colleen McCullough seems to have found an excellent solution to the problem in her recent Roman books, beginning with *The First Man in Rome.* As with Shaara, McCullough deals almost completely with characters from verifiable history, often going to primary sources and reading the letters, diaries and speeches in their original Latin. Between her ability as a storyteller and the richness of her subject, there is no lack of interesting characters or events.

However, when confronted with the problem of explaining to the reader things unique to that time and place—late Roman Republic during the last century before Christ—she came up with a splendid solution.

The first 85 to 90 percent of the book is story text, while the last 10 to 15 percent is a Glossary in which she explains all manner of things from how intensely superstitious Romans were to the overwhelming importance of family dignity. These are things that, like the Oriental need to save face, shape people's lives and influence historic decisions, but unless explained make little or no sense to the contemporary western reader.

With the addition of this glossary, where even bits of background history are listed, McCullough seems to have created a truly *interactive book* in publishable format. The reader who wants to understand the forces behind the scenes will go to the glossary for that information, and the fan who'd rather be swept away by the adventure, romance or political intrigue can happily stick with the fictional narrative.

BIOGRAPHY AS FICTION:
THE AGONY AND THE ECSTASY

Irving Stone's first biography in novel form, *Lust for Life*, took the world by storm when it was published in 1934. At that time Vincent Van Gogh's paintings had already attracted acclaim, but his personal life and tragedy were much less known. Stone's work helped make him a symbol of the struggling visionary.

The notion of fictionalizing an actual, historical person's life was not entirely new: Somerset Maugham had done the same with Gauguin's life in *The Moon and Six Pence* in 1919, though he changed the names of all involved. But Stone's treatment of Van Gogh went over big, and Stone became one of the most popular exponents of the technique, going on to do books on Freud, John and Jessie Fremont and, of course, Michelangelo.

There are several reasons to write the biography of a real person as a historical novel: You may want the freedom to bring out some hidden facet of the person's life or character that you can't substantiate with factual proof but have good cause to think worthwhile; the character may be privy to or have a particular insight about a situation that hasn't been explored before; or they might exemplify a specific era, as Michelangelo did the Renaissance.

Some biographers use the novel form because the people they are writing about have become sacred cows and it takes a totally new approach to make them human again. Gore Vidal's *Lincoln* is one such work, and though his research appears to be impeccable, there was quite a stir when the book came out in 1984 because Vidal portrayed Lincoln as a common politician who grew into the office, rather than serving up the semisainted savior so many writers offer us. Vidal seems to thoroughly enjoy taking either villain or hero and recasting them in human, three-dimensional form, and as a novelist he has become a master of this. *Burr* and *Julian* are two other examples of Vidal's far-ranging interests.

There are some major pitfalls in turning a biography into a novel (whether positive or negative in your approach to your subject), particularly if you're a first-time novelist. If you choose an already famous person, there are bound to be scholars who know a great deal more about the character than you're likely to find out in a few months' research, so you're in danger of launching your career as a writer only to meet heaps of scorn by the establishment and/or reviewers.

Then, too, if the characters are famous, there may already be so many books on the subject, another one by you would just get lost. At one point I thought about doing one on Richard III, that much maligned monarch whom Shakespeare turned into the quintessential villain. Then I saw the list of how many books there were already in print about him (fiction and nonfiction) and realized that almost every day of his life could be accounted for, sometimes right down to the hour. This meant I would have to be doubly accurate in the timing and placing of my characters, and I wasn't sure I wanted to put that much energy into it.

If I'd had some flaming inspiration that would have made my approach different from anyone else's, if I'd found something new to say about Richard or a new way to say it, I probably would have made the effort. But genius didn't strike on that subject, so I've never followed it up.

And that brings up the most important questions I ask myself when I start a book. WHY do I want to do it? I firmly believe that neither the book nor the author escape the writing process unscathed. If the book and its creator are the same when it's over as when the idea first took shape, something hasn't worked. Therefore the project better be one you believe in; if it's not, you've wasted years of your life and probably produced a pretty flat product as well. So look at why you want to devote yourself to that particular story or character, and try to recognize what you'll be getting out of it, besides a (hopefully) new career and major check.

Then come the questions, WHO will want to read it? and WHAT MAKES IT UNIQUE? I didn't discover the Arthurian stories until I was well into my twenties, and then it took another two decades of wishing I had some new approach to the Matter of Britain before it dawned on me no one had, in 1980, looked at the story from Guinevere's point of view. The moment I realized that, I knew what my first novel would be.

How you answer these questions is totally up to you. No one need know you've even contemplated them, but I strongly suggest you do so, because no matter what conclusions you come to, if you're going to launch yourself into a full-scale historical fiction project, you'll be using up lots of time, thought and energy.

And you're going to need enough familiarity with the era to make it plausible, which is where the matter of research comes in.

CHAPTER THREE

First Things First

IS RESEARCH THAT IMPORTANT?

Absolutely.

The classic advice for beginning novelists is "write what you know about." There are several reasons for this, chief among them being that if you're familiar with something to the core, you'll convey it more smoothly to the reader.

As a novelist you have an implicit contract with your audience. They give you their attention, time and money in order to be entertained, informed and maybe presented with a new idea or two. They agree, upon opening your book, to suspend their own reality in order to enter your world and follow your story.

This holds true if you're writing Regency romance, a western saga or contemporary fiction; the readers' sense of time and place, as well as the cohesiveness of the world they are encountering, all depend on you as the storyteller knowing what you're talking about.

Whether you're another Eileen Goudge writing about contemporary society or Mary Renault specializing in ancient Greece, every novelist evokes a specific world for the reader. Goudge writes for an audience that knows today's fashions, foods and mores as well as she does; Renault's readers experience a world vastly different from their own. Yet both authors create fully believable environments that don't detract from the reader's interest in the characters, but do add a specific and special flavor to the story.

How do they do it? They get to know the world they're writing about so thoroughly it's almost second nature to them—and therefore second nature to the characters. Even if these authors were alive during the specific time, chances are they would do some thumbing through magazines, skimming of contemporary books and listening to appropriate music just to freshen their memories. In other words, they do their research.

Sometimes people say, "But it's only a novel, after all . . . surely you don't need to do research when you can make it up as you go along."

There are several reasons why that doesn't work. First of all, why reinvent the wheel? You're going to have to figure out how your characters fasten that garment sometime . . . a broach, a belt, a tie, a clasp? Often it's a lot easier, to say nothing of quicker, to look it up than it is to extrapolate what they *might* have done. (Doll clubs are excellent sources for this sort of fashion information, as are theatrical groups that have a costumer interested in the development of clothing and costumes. Don't hesitate to call and explain your predicament. Very possibly they'll be so delighted that someone outside their circle appreciates their expertise, they'll track down the answer to your problem within twenty-four hours.)

Secondly, no matter how obscure your time frame, at least a few of your readers are going to be well versed in it. That may even be what attracted them to your book to begin with. And they're going to know when you've tried to wing it, even if the average reader doesn't. When that happens, you've just stepped into the biggest bear trap facing historical authors—anachronism.

BEWARE THOSE STEELY JAWS

Every author wants to capture the audience's total attention and avoid any intrusion, doubt or confusion that distracts from the story. Suddenly stumbling over a detail that the reader knows is incorrect—or worse, inconsistent—breaks that contract between story giver and receiver.

Anachronisms can be as little and annoying as a popcorn husk scratching at the back of your throat or as big as a black hole in space. Certainly they can undermine your career because they shatter the pact you've made with your reader.

Say you're writing about Napoleon's retreat from Moscow and you have your poor starving French soldier delight in finding a patch of wild onions no one else has dug up. A good half of your readers will know that death march took place in the heart of winter, with blizzards and death by freezing being as much a threat as starvation. There is no way anyone could dig anything out of the ground when it was covered with ice and snow.

That's a fairly obvious lapse. On the more subtle but just as devastating level, you can't have Galileo walking around with a kerosene lantern (kerosene not having been discovered back then) or your 1846 heroine listening to the bullfrogs in a California pond (bullfrogs didn't live here then—it was the French who introduced them during the gold rush in order to have a handy snack on hand when they didn't want to go hunting bigger game). Little things that no one notices, right? Wrong.

Not only will they notice, they will write you letters pointing out the error of your ways. Sometimes these letters are pleasant but firm in tone, and sometimes they are downright vinegary, particularly if you've put our foot in your reader's turf. But it's the ones you don't hear from that are worrisome; they may just decide not to read your future books on the basis of some silly anachronism that slipped by you in this one. Consequently it's worthwhile covering as many bases as you can, if only to avoid unnecessary brickbats.

(Remember that this is particularly true if you're writing about a fairly recent era, such as World War II, which some of your audience may remember from firsthand experience. If you mention nylon panty hose during that time, any editor who's half-awake will turn you down flat, both because panty hose hadn't been developed yet and, more importantly, all nylon, which had only just been invented, was conscripted for military use in parachutes and such and wasn't available for the citizens at home.)

Another problem with anachronisms is that they can crop up in a hundred ways—because you didn't go to the actual location, or forgot to check what plants were native, or slipped out of context in your word choices. They are the one hazard that can creep in during planning, development or writing, and you need to be constantly alert to their potential presence.

Lest you think I'm being *too* stringent in alerting you to this problem, I've heard too many people say (about movies as well as books), "I really liked the idea, but then suddenly such and such happened, and I couldn't get back into it after that." Surely you don't want to lose a reader just for the lack of a little more research and verification!

HOW MUCH RESEARCH IS ENOUGH?

That depends on the style of the individual writer, how important the historical setting is to the story, and whether you enjoy doing research.

Some authors put in several evenings with the encyclopedia, either at the library or online, and consider it enough. That's probably sufficient for picking up a few highlights here and there to suggest the era—gaslights on the street, the clop of hooves on cobblestone, etc. If your book relies heavily on character rather than historical era and ambiance, that may be enough. But if you're writing something that could only have taken place in your chosen milieu, chances are you'll need to put in more than just a couple of hours of research.

On the other extreme, there are those who spend years on a project, delving into all sorts of details and sources with the enthusiasm of a bloodhound on a fresh scent. Sometimes that's necessary if you're searching out a difficult-to-find bit of information—burial customs of sixth-century Saxons in a particular area of Britain, for instance. But beware—too often the feeling that you need to do just a little more research becomes a handy excuse to keep from writing the book itself. When that happens, the would-be novelist never quite gets around to writing the text.

Don't feel bad if you've been thinking about a project for a long time, however. Although I originally expected to put in six months of research and six months of writing for the Guinevere book, it was actually a little over three full years between my original concept and my typing *Chapter 1* at the top of a blank screen. Colleen McCullough did thirteen years of research and planning before writing a single word on her first Roman book. In her case everything is carefully planned out beforehand, as she says she rarely even rearranges sequences, for instance.

All told I put in eleven years of actual research and writing on the Guinevere trilogy and was confirming dates and circumstances right up to the last moment of typesetting on the final volume. But considering that Gwen started supporting me in the fifth year, and has done so more or less for the last decade, I don't think it was time wasted, either for myself or my readers. So I suggest you keep a firm eye on how long you are willing to devote to research, and then get on with it.

Most authors, of course, fall someplace between the cursory visit to the library and the all-out consuming lifestyle of the professional researcher. Ken Follett and Parke Godwin spend a year or more per book, often researching and writing as they go along. James

Michener was said to hire whole teams of researchers, but few of us have that option. Besides, you must have some interest in history or you wouldn't be writing a historical novel. So indulge that interest by getting to know more about your chosen era. Probably a good percentage of what you learn will never actually get into print, but the knowledge you'll gain will add to the depth and dimension of your work and, hopefully, the size of your sale.

(If you positively hate research, stick with contemporary novels set in your own hometown; nothing wrong with that, after all, and better you enjoy your work than slog through something you really dislike doing.)

HISTORICAL EVENTS

In general you'll be looking for two specific kinds of information: the factual history of the time and place, and the daily lifestyle of the people living in that time and place. Eventually, of course, you'll be creating a synthesis of both in order to tell the most believable story you can.

For me, studying the lifestyle of an era is sort of ongoing, while learning what events shaped which years requires specific concentration. Both areas can be researched through books, on the Internet, by watching videos or engaging in correspondence, and all of it is basic information that needs to become part of your personal database.

Margaret Mitchell's *Gone With the Wind* came easily to her in part because her father was an ardent student of Georgia history, so she grew up hearing about it from an academic point of view. As a small girl she listened for hours to old ladies recounting their personal experiences in Atlanta during the Civil War and the aftermath of Sherman's march to the sea. And later she spent time with the old veterans who sat on the steps in the sun, reliving their days fighting for Dixie.

It was, therefore, something she already knew a good deal about and could use as an integral part of her story.

And use it she did, from Rhett's dashing off to join the Rebels after helping Scarlett escape Atlanta, to Scarlett's near starvation following the aftermath, which leads her to vow she will never be hungry again.

These are excellent examples of actual history being used to shape fictional characters. None of the characters caused any of the events to happen, but they certainly did react to them, and took us as readers right along with them.

(It's interesting to note that in spite of Mitchell's thorough grounding in the material, she still spent hours poring over newspaper accounts of the time, as well as visiting various Civil War sites around Atlanta while she was in the midst of writing the story.)

If the era you've chosen includes such cataclysmic happenings as a civil war or your characters have access to big, sweeping events full of dramatic promise or threat, by all means use them. That is, after all, one of the reasons people read historical fiction.

Not that you have to always go for the obvious. One of the delights of research is the discovery of either an obscure event or a new perspective that dovetails wonderfully with your story. Parke Godwin's *Sherwood* contains an excellent example of this. Early on he focuses on the battle at York, which followed William the Conqueror's invasion of Hastings by several years. Hastings in 1066 is the more familiar scene, but as Godwin delved into the historical accounts, he found the seeds of treachery and deceit in the York battle that would do more to sustain his plot than the all-out conquest at Hastings could. Also, York is closer to Sherwood Forest and therefore keeps the action in the more familiar locale.

So remember, take the time to explore the whole landscape of your era before choosing what best serves your story's needs. It doesn't have to be the explosion of Krakatoa to be important to your characters, and you may find your story gaining depth or even a new direction because of some smaller historical happening you run across in the course of your research.

LIFESTYLES

The second area of research has to do with everyday living: How did your people manage on a daily basis? Would your heroine sit astride her horse or ride sidesaddle? What kind of public conveyances were there, if any? How did they cook, light, heat or clean their living spaces? Were women segregated into separate quarters as in Roman days, or did they have free access to streets, shops and other public gathering places?

And one needs to ask similar questions for the location as well as the era: What kinds of food were most prevalent—fish near the shore, dried meats and beans in the drier, inland areas, fruits and vegetables in the lusher, more moderate climes?

Don't forget, it's only in our lifetimes that food from around the world has become available in the local market; fresh pineapples were unheard of outside of Hawaii, mangos or papaya were only known in chutneys and conserves, and my own mother wouldn't buy fresh mushrooms when they did appear in the market because she was sure they had been collected wild, and everyone knows you might get a toadstool by mistake.

Not only were food sources and types more limited prior to World War II, preservation was different as well. Widespread refrigeration (both for shipping and storing), and frozen foods are mid-twentieth-century phenomena.

As recently as the early 1900s you never cooked more than you thought you could eat at one meal because there was no way to keep it from spoiling, and up through the 1940s the heavy tread of the iceman, a big block of ice slung onto the rubber pad on his shoulder, was as familiar in urban areas as the clatter of the milkman delivering the glass bottles to the doorstep in the predawn.

We are so used to controlling climate and light for farm animals as well as ourselves, it comes as a shock to realize how much we've tampered with nature's basic rhythms. Both eggs and milk were far more seasonal than they are now, beginning in the spring after the cow calved and the hens started laying and ending in the fall when shorter days told the chickens not to produce any more eggs and the cow's milk dried up due to lack of green fodder. Indeed, salting butter was something done specifically for those crocks you put into the coolest spot—often the springhouse—and hoped the salt preserved it through the winter. Sweet (unsalted) butter was "fresh" and only available during milk-producing seasons.

Since food was so basic to survival, much time and energy went into capturing, preparing and preserving it. But for women there were also the "distaff" chores, the distaff being a tool used in spinning, which was considered women's work in most western societies. Without spinning there was no thread from which to weave fabric and clothe the body; no twine for nets, bags, snares, rope and other products of string; no soft, thick yarn for blankets, sweaters and other heavy coverings. So women in the preindustrial age spent many hours gathering and retting flax for linen, washing and carding fleece for wool and dying, weaving and embroidering countless miles of fabric for tapestries to cut down on the drafts, decorate the chapels or make into banners with which to lead armies into war. Unless your characters are among the very rich and privileged, they would be doing some of these things—or at least overseeing them.

For men there were not only the multiple aspects of hunting (Did they use falcons? hounds? bow and arrow or musket?), but also the manufacture and care of tools, whether for farm or war or hunting. Even if they were hunting for sport rather than food, if they didn't fletch their own arrows or hone their own spear tips, they would make sure to find other people who did a good job for them.

Among the working classes, particularly farmers, there was always something that needed to be done, from the cleaning of hoes, shovels and plows to the dressing and repairing of tack used with horses or oxen.

All of these represent the daily aspects of living that need to be taken into consideration as you envision your characters going about their story. Often they can be woven in as bits of "business," something a character does while talking to someone else, etc., which not only adds color and authenticity, but also helps keep your prose from the flatness of "he said, she said."

For instance, in *Guinevere: the Legend in Autumn,* I used Gwen's need to check Camelot's pharmacy with the healer, Nimue, as a chance to talk privately (such vitals would be kept under lock and key in a rarely used place). As they were checking and sniffing herbs and potions for quantity and freshness, Gwen notes that she fears Morgan has not abandoned the idea of destroying Arthur.

> "Probably not abandoned," Nimue agreed, holding up a vial of rosemary oil. "But getting rid of a popular king is hard work . . ."

In this way the two women further the story and keep up the ambiance at the same time.

Every era and culture has attitudes and activities that are peculiar to it, so look on your research as both background and treasure hunt that can give you color as well as content and make the difference between a good solid sale and a ho-hum refusal.

GETTING STARTED

It's important to begin your research early, even before you have a complete story line. Once you know the era and/or locale you want to use, start studying it.

There are several reasons for this: Not only is this the matrix for your story, if you're still flexible about plot and characters your research will suggest people or situations that you wouldn't have come up with on your own; for example, a law against tinkers in Ireland may provide you with a whole new plot device, or the discovery of an antique photograph of a man with a pet bear at a gold camp may add a new character to your cast. At the very least a hundred subplots will come to mind as you go along, if you keep your eyes open for the perfect place or event that can be used to illuminate some aspect of your story or characters.

WHO DOES WHAT, WHEN

One of the first things to take care of is setting up your time line— who is where, when, why and doing what. I find this a handy chart to have for every book, simply because it helps me keep track of where everyone is at any given point in the story. I lay it out on a linear basis, using several large pages of newsprint side by side, with the dates at the top and different characters in different colors marching across. (The color coding makes it easier to read at a glance.) This is also a good place to put, down one side margin, the estimated birth dates of all the characters; it's amazing how helpful such a list is as your story progresses.

Early research and time charts will also help you avoid disasters in the middle of your writing. There are few things more frustrating than setting up a scene only to realize it couldn't possibly work that way once you actually get to it.

For instance, when I was planning *Sierra* I had an entire branch of the saga dealing with a Chinese woman who has lost both husband and teenaged sons in the civil strife of Canton. Seeking a new life, she comes to California as a mail-order bride, only to be thrown into one of the cribs in Chinatown. She escapes the world of prostitution once she realizes she's pregnant, and that child— a boy—eventually goes to work for the railroad, thereby tieing in this branch with the rest of the book. It was a good device that introduced all sorts of things: another female voice in a world that was predominantly male; the power and courage of impending motherhood; the cosmopolitan but brutal nature of San Francisco in its early days.

Then I discovered the majority of Chinese women weren't

tricked into coming to California until 1852. Even if my widow got pregnant immediately, the boy would be barely eleven when I wanted him on the railroad—probably too little and too young, even in an era without child-labor laws. In the end that entire portion of the book was dropped, but at least I recognized the problems before the actual writing started!

So get to your research early, stay flexible and keep an open mind for possible new story ideas, character conflict and opportunities as you go along. Believe me, it's worth it in the long run.

RESOURCES

For academic information, libraries, bookstores, museums and magazine subscriptions are the best places to start. Make it a point to get acquainted with your local librarians—they can be immensely helpful. Most libraries will take reference questions over the phone if they aren't too busy, and they can track down everything from when brass beds were introduced in this country to the availability of a specific book footnoted in something you've recently read, all with a simple phone call.

I personally prefer to buy books whenever possible. For one thing, if you wake up at three o'clock in the morning with a great new idea for how to get rid of a particularly trying character, it's nice to be able to reach for the poisonous plants book right then. Helpful as most librarians are, they can't be expected to get out of bed and open the facilities for you in the middle of the night just because inspiration struck.

My own personal libraries for my major works grew to hundreds of titles and have included such things as forestry pamphlets on the habits of hedgehogs in Britain (for the Guinevere books) and recipes for sourdough biscuits from mining camps (for *Sierra*). If you follow suit, it can become a sizeable investment, running to thousands of dollars a year. But every book, video or magazine that relates to what you're doing can be deducted from your taxable income, which is a help in the long run.

For years now, various publishers have brought out books dealing with the daily lifestyles of times and cultures as diverse as ancient Greece and Restoration England. Some of the older ones are dated in their presentation, but their information, is still valid. And Writer's Digest Books' "Everyday Life" series is particularly useful since it's geared specifically to the needs of historical authors. And there are treasures by individual writers; for instance, an excellent source for medieval information is Dorothy Hartley's *Lost Country Life*, which has the additional benefit of being so well written it's an absolute delight to read just for fun.

Whenever you go to a bookstore, be it new, used or in a museum, always check the history, anthropology and travel sections, as well as the more specialized subjects. You'll find there are books on just about everything; map making, range wars, herbal medicine, obscure political references in the works of Jonathan Swift. You may have to do some extra poking and prying for some of your subject matter, but chances are if you're curious about it, someone has already written a book on it.

When I started *Sierra*, I was afraid I was going to have to wade through years of legislative notes looking for information about the fight between farmers and miners over the damage hydraulic mining was doing to the valley. But a trip to my local library turned up a book called *Gold vs. Grain* that dealt with exactly what I wanted to know. So don't overlook the obvious just because it's obvious.

Sometimes you'll run across mail-order book groups, such as the History Book Club, that specialize in history-oriented works, or various book outlets that send out their catalogs every few months and cover an enormous range of subjects at remaindered prices. At least it's worth scanning their current offerings, as you'll occasionally find a jewel.

And don't forget university presses. Often their works are more available through mail-order catalogs than libraries or stores, but they have a wealth of information about very specific subjects and are usually the most reliable sources for academic information.

Then, too, there are the books designed specifically for people who collect a particular thing, such as *A Guide Book of United States Coins*, *Lanterns That Lit Our World* or *The Vanishing American Barber Shop*.

Originally designed to help catalog and price the collectibles, they often provide insights, pictures and detailed information you wouldn't find anyplace else. They can be expensive if you buy them at a collector's fair, for instance, but are often worth the price. And if you run across them at a garage sale, so much the better.

By all means photocopy the bibliographies in the backs of such books or make note of those works that are mentioned in footnotes. Often as you go along you'll run across one or two titles that everyone else references; obviously it's a seminal work in that particular area and might be of help to you as well, so don't hesitate to check it out yourself.

Magazines also cover quite a range of subjects, and some of the best are pure labors of love, rarely available in stores and often put out by a devoted team of fanatics who do it more for love than money, such as *The Californians* or *Dogtown Territorial Quarterly*, both of which deal with California's history, or *Quontum et Futurus*, a quarterly published specifically for King Arthur scholars. If you find magazines, newsletters or quarterlies that specialize in your field or era, consider subscribing, and if they do reviews, they'd be naturals to receive review copies of your finished product.

Maps are another source of information. How long would it take to go from this point to that by horse? Ox-drawn wagon? Infantry march? Is the road straight and fast or winding and slow? Are there major impediments such as rivers to cross, mountains to scale, lakes to skirt? One whole series of British Ordinance maps includes things like castle ruins, stone circles and abbeys, as well as footpaths, the elevation of any particular hill and occasionally battlefields. In the course of my work on Guinevere, I slowly acquired more than three-quarters of all the Ordinance maps, and while I may not have used every one every day, when I needed to check something out I was thankful to have them as they are frightfully expensive to purchase here, and hard to find besides.

SOCIETIES

Keep your eye out for special societies that deal with your particular subject or genre. These can range from Western Writers of America to the Richard III Society. There are bottle collectors, bagpipers, barbershop historians, old time fire-engine companies, barrel-makers and steam-engine buffs all over the English-speaking world, and they each have organizations. For the most part they are delighted to find another person interested in their hobby, vocation or obsession and will usually welcome a curious researcher with open arms.

Groups such as these often have libraries that focus on their specific subjects. The J. Porter Shaw library at the Maritime Museum in San Francisco is one such place that can fill you in on just about anything you need to know about American maritime history. Usually you'll find individual members who specialize in specific areas; many states have Civil War organizations, which do everything from roundtable discussions to reenactments of cannon fire. Their members can tell you all you'll ever need to know about black powder, battlefield medicine, dentistry and drummer boys . . . or they can give you the name of another member in another chapter who can. Just remember, if Jean Auel could find a flint knapping specialist for her *Clan of the Cave Bear* books, you can find whatever you need, somewhere.

Don't forget that these special interest groups often have conferences. My hometown hosts a regional convention for the collectors of insulators from telegraph and telephone lines, for instance. And yes, I did find a book on the early day telegraphers that provided much needed information on early telegraph offices.

USING A MODERN NET FOR HISTORICAL FISHES

Although the Internet is not a society in itself, it can be called on to supply information from magazines, museums, newspapers, libraries, special organizations and societies. Here you will encounter experts (real and self-appointed), scholars and amateur archaeologists, historians, travel buffs and fans who are *specifically* knowledgeable about or interested in your era, locale or subject. As a research tool it is unsurpassed, making it possible to tap into the collected knowledge of all mankind. And, if that's not enough, when you've got a question that's stumping you completely—such as the name of the Gothic leader who took over Italy in the mid-sixth Century and wrote a book of laws for both Romans and Goths—you can fling it out into cyberspace, and someone will have the answer for you, possibly immediately.

There are numerous services to help the beginner, such as America OnLine, CompuServe or Prodigy, which charge monthly fees to help you access the Net. Subscribing to one of these may be well worth it if you're just getting started, unless you have a computer wizard in the family, living next door or only a phone call away. For those who are already computer literate and comfortable with adventuring, direct service providers and a browser are cheaper and possibly quicker.

There are numerous books on the subject, ranging from specifics about individual services, such as Tom Lichty's *America OnLine's Internet,* to Ellen Metter's *The Writer's Ultimate Research Guide.*

REMEMBER THAT TIME IS MONEY, particularly on your computer. More than one researcher, newly captivated by the incredible amount of information, discussion and inspiration the Net offers, has suddenly found telephone and credit card bills soaring. On the other hand, this tool not only puts the wealth of human knowledge at your fingertips, it can also help you promote your book once you're published; all those sources, professionals and fellow history buffs are likely to be thrilled for you and begin asking for your work in their nearest bookstores.

If you don't have the wherewithal to get on the Net or do not have a computer, take a look at your local library; many have public access to the Net. Some, in both urban and rural areas, allow patrons blocks of time on it at little or no charge.

Also, keep in mind that, depending on how much you use it for other things, much of the cost of going (and staying) online is tax deductible.

MUSEUMS

Just because we're moving into the twenty-first century doesn't mean those old standbys—museums—should be ignored. They come in all sizes and locations, from a corner in an old firehouse to grand municipal structures full of galleries and exhibit halls. There's a wealth of information in them, both big and small, and they cover an amazing variety of subjects.

Lots of areas have nature centers that catalog, depict and display what the locale was like originally, before modern technology brought about major changes. Others honor specific cultural heritages, from Native Americans to immigrant groups, while still others house collections, histories and books on dolls, antique tractors, the development of oil wells, railroads, airplanes or space exploration. I've found folk-art museums, lace museums, even a tattoo museum in my browsings, and most all provide the kind of glimpse into another era the historical novelist is looking for.

Many museums have docents to guide you through their displays. Try taking the same tour with different docents; each one will have a particular specialty and interest that the others may overlook. My day at the Roman ruins in Bath included three different docent tours and tons of new information from each. So if the subject or locale fascinates you, don't figure you've gotten all the information from just one voice.

And by all means tell the museum people about your project.

Often they will know about or have items that are too specialized, fragile or rare to be out on general display, but they are happy to bring them out for someone with a specific interest, such as you. Even just telling them you're working on a novel involving their area or a character represented in their museum will generate all sorts of response, and you may be showered with an abundance of leads, photocopied pages and the names of other people to contact on the subject.

AUTHORS AND AUTHORITIES

Once you've gotten a handle on your material, don't hesitate to write to those authors whose work you have found most useful.

Everyone likes to hear from a satisfied reader, and if you have an additional question that's gone unanswered, the specialists may be able to help you. Sometimes they'll provide further contacts, a new perspective or some little detail that didn't fit in their books, but might in yours. Certainly it can't hurt to ask, if it's done politely.

There is one caveat, however. NEVER contact a specialist with an amateur question. Wait until you truly have a good working knowledge of the material before you write to such people, and always begin by telling them how much their work helped you with yours. IF they encourage you to correspond further, you might well establish a new friendship, of sorts. I've not only met other authors that way, I've also become friends with several people who simply wrote to me as fans, not as hopeful authors themselves.

Some specialists are open to reading a few pages of *finished* manuscript to check for errors. You need to feel that one out carefully: If an authority agrees to read a particular segment, be sure to send him ONLY the portion that deals with his specialty—dueling habits in the Old West, for instance. DO NOT send the prior chapters that set up the duel, as that's plot development, and you shouldn't expect him to read the whole book. DO be sure to include a return envelope with enough postage that he can simply slip your pages (marked on the margins, usually) back into the post for you as soon as he's read them.

The most common way to reach an author is by sending your letter to her "In Care of" the publisher, whose address is usually in the front of the book. The one problem with it is that sometimes those letters get delayed, fall behind desks, get routed to the wrong person or otherwise disappear into the mysterious byways of big-time publishers, and if they emerge at all, it can be months later.

Frequently authors will include where they live in the blurbs at the ends of their books, and you can inquire from the telephone company if there's a phone number and address listed. Or you can check them out in your library's copy of *Contemporary Authors*, as they might well be listed there. Keep in mind that it is more thoughtful to write than to call, however, as they can answer at their leisure.

So much for research through books, videos, the Net and so forth. How long you go on in this mode depends largely on you and your needs, desires, time, fears and finances. Just remember that research by itself can become a trap—a delightful one, to be sure, but a trap if you use it as an excuse for not writing. More than one hopeful author remains a wanna-be because they're so busy collecting all their information, they never get around to using it. View it as a tool, and you'll be a lot farther along in the game than most.

CHAPTER FOUR

Corralling Your Material

There are few things more frustrating than knowing you have what you need, but you can't lay your hands on it. By the same token, reaching mentally for the name of a special river or the year that earthquake devastated the region you're writing about and discovering you can't find it can be absolutely infuriating.

Even if you do have access to all the books you've read on the subject, looking up specifics is only possible if the author has thought to index things in the way that you remember them. It's amazing how many things in a book don't get listed in the index, to say nothing of the number of books that aren't indexed at all, so always check that part of a book before buying it.

TAKING NOTES

One of the best solutions is to keep notes as you go along. Always have a binder or clipboard with paper handy whenever you sit down to read; it may slow down your reading, but how else are you going to sift out the things you want to use? At the same time you can note any new points and ideas (P&Is) that come to you, and after you've filed your pages in appropriate folders, you'll be able look up what you want with a minimum of fuss.

If your book logically breaks down into several sections, either geographically or timewise, you might want to use different colored papers when researching the different aspects. Lined pads can be bought in pink, blue and white as well as yellow now; color coding your information makes it much easier to organize, and when looking for something, a quick scan will ascertain if you're searching the right pile . . . i.e. Trojan notes in one color, Greek notes in another.

When I take notes, I put the full title of the book in the upper right-hand corner and write out the author's whole name under it on the first page, thereby assuring that I can track down the actual tome in the future, if need be. It's amazing how often you think you noted all the pertinent material, but when you actually write the story, some little detail is missing, and you need to return to the source for further information.

I also put the page number from the book in the left-hand margin, on the same line as the note; it speeds up the confirmation process immensely.

When something really tasty comes along, I put a big arrow in the left margin to signify that this is a choice bit of information which fits in wonderfully with my story line. And if it has led to a new idea or plot twist, I generally note that with a "P&I" in the same margin or put it on a separate page headed "Points and Ideas."

Once I've finished reading, I collect all the relevant pages and stash them in a folder. My Guinevere trilogy left me with an enormous stack of manilla folders bulging with notes: Celtic Place-Names, Saxon Gods and Religious Rites, Roman Towns, Forts and Ruins, Scottish Food, British Mineral Resources. And, of course, there was a folder on each character in the legend as well.

These files (and their sometimes tattered contents) will serve you in good stead if you (1) remember to file things in the appropriate place and (2) take the time to browse through them occasionally as your manuscript progresses. Not only will they keep you well grounded in your place and era, they can provide a jumpstart for your enthusiasm if something intervened and you had to put the project away for a while.

All of this may seem unwieldy, and it can take a day or two just to go through from beginning to end, but it allows you to recall details and color from your research that might otherwise have gotten lost, and providing you keep current on your filing, most anything can be retrieved without too much trouble.

COMPUTER VS. PAPER

Technology is marvelous, if it furthers your work. Standing at a museum display, madly scribbling in my spiral notebook often makes me wish I had a portable scanner. At least it could record all that text curators work so hard to put up as part of their exhibits.

On the other hand, scanning in all sorts of information doesn't help if you don't take the time to read it carefully. The very process of collecting research often gives rise to the most creative notions, and if it's the electronic impulses of the computer that are getting fired up rather than the electrons in your brain, your story isn't going to benefit.

For quick retrieval, of course, a computer is ideal; just specify what you want to find, and assuming you've entered it in an organized fashion, bingo! There it is on the screen—the date Benjamin Franklin flew his kite, the first building to have an elevator in New York or the name of Sacagawea's papoose.

This does, however, presuppose that you're already computer literate, understand the finer aspects of organizing databases and have the time for entering everything you might want to retrieve. If you meet the first two qualifications, it's no doubt useful to make the time to put your research into the computer. But if you are starting from scratch, be aware of the fact that you may be putting aside months just to get up to speed, much less getting familiar enough with the tool to find it useful. In making this kind of decision, it's important to take into consideration finances (buying a computer can be expensive), support systems (whether in the form of a friend, relative or local user's group) and the other basic variables: How much do you really want this, do you have the time to learn to use it and do you foresee enough projects down the road to make such an investment worthwhile?

As noted, if you're on the Internet, the world is at your fingertips. Or you can find a library that offers the use of computers that have access to the Net. This last approach is an excellent way to learn to use this modern Aladdin's lamp with the help of a professional available if the genie gets stuck. Certainly it's worth seeing what your local library has along this line.

Even if you're already set up for and familiar with the Internet, I still suggest downloading and printing out whatever you specifically want to keep. Sitting and reading printed material may be an old-fashioned habit left over from the days of typewriters, but for most of us it jogs the mind's creativity better than something on the screen does, unless that something is a video presentation.

TV DOCUMENTARIES
Speaking of electronics, don't forget plain old TV. Since the proliferation of cable channels, there are many excellent educational

and historical documentaries to be seen. These productions sometimes provide insights or perspectives you might not get from other
sources and often have a remarkable range of visuals. They may
also have maps and photos that are not generally in print or available to the public.

The variety of such programs is truly amazing, and being able
to study visuals of your subject can add depth and color to your
writing, particularly where wild animals are concerned. People living in a nonurban environment up to the end of the last century
would be sharing their world with any number of animals we now
see only in zoos: wolves, grizzlies, prong horn antelope and buffalo,
just to name a few from the United States. Although many of the
nature programs on television deal with exotic animals that will
only help you if your novel is set in the rain forests of South
America, you'll find some that give you an in-depth look at more
common critters or places in America.

Big gray wolves, although not a problem in the western portion
of the United States, have been a threat almost everywhere else
for much of mankind's history. The wolf attack sequence in Willa
Cather's *My Antonia* brings that home in a most chilling way; she
conveys both the ferocity of the animals and the fragility of human-
kind—even when in groups and using vehicles—and the event is,
understandably, a turning point in the lives of two minor
characters.

Naturally you'll want to check to be sure of the range and location of any particular animal you're planning to use; most collections of bird or mammal books include maps that show the distribution of the subject, whether it's a permanent resident or
migratory visitor, and if it's the latter, when it can be expected and
why.

Although TV documentaries aren't as easy to use for quick reference, nature programs do give you color, action and close-up observation of the animals themselves that are almost as good as
being there. For instance, do foxes have whiskers, and are the
pupils of goats' eyes really horizontal rather than vertical? (Yes to
both, which gives each of them a particularly expressive look.)

By all means record these programs on your VCR. If you don't
have one, get one. As long as you use it for research rather than
entertainment, you can deduct all related costs from your taxable
income, and the VCR will pay for itself many times over when
compared to the cost of buying individual programs, or even whole

sets. If you check the TV listings regularly, you'll probably find any number of specials or documentaries that relate to your region or your era, and a library of recorded visuals is as useful as a library of books.

Television biographies can be another source of inspiration and information. Nowadays they range from Attila the Hun to Marilyn Monroe, and while you may not be incorporating those specific personalities in your novel, a good biography will provide information about the surrounding era. Naturally if it's recent enough to be captured on film or tape, you'll have access to primary source material: Just what did Jackie Kennedy's pillbox hats look like, anyhow? And if it's more ancient, you'll probably see close-ups of museum items that would require a worldwide trek to see in person.

When taping such programs, make sure to record the credits; usually there are a list of archival sources—museums, scholars, national parks, etc.—that can become useful to you if you need to write to one with a specific question. Again, remember that professionals generally enjoy sharing their knowledge, but don't pester them with amateur questions you could find the answer to in any encyclopedia.

BUILD MORE BOOKCASES!

While different authors' needs vary tremendously, most of us want to have our research material on hand when we need it and available when we want it, regardless of the hour of day or night. Consequently we build up reference libraries that, whether small or large, are likely to be a mixed blessing; outside of actual research trips to specific locales, books are likely to be your biggest expense, and where to put them your second biggest problem.

(If you're content with two solid resource books and a few magazines, fine. But if you find yourself acquiring a considerably bigger library, you don't need to feel like a freak; as Jean Auel said when she checked out a stack of books almost too high to carry home just to do some research for a short story on a Stone-Age girl, she should have guessed she was in for more than a 5,000-word quickie.)

If your budget is limited, by all means get used books. With the price of paper escalating every day, it makes economic sense to recycle books, and it's more environmentally sound as well. Also, older books are that much closer to your era, and though they may not have all the newly developed theories that modern technology (such as pollen analysis) makes possible, they often have a more humane approach to what would have been important to your characters. For instance, I found a memoir, printed in the 1920s, that chronicles an old man's childhood and youth in Manhattan during the 1850s and 1860s. First-person, eyewitness, prime source material—all for fifty cents at a garage sale.

Another great source of used books is the Friends of the Library (FOL) sales held monthly in most areas. FOLs are local support organizations set up to make money for the libraries. The bulk of the books are donated by library users rather than being discards from the library itself and will range from dog-eared romances to the occasional mint condition jewel. Here in California the prices range from a quarter per book up to a dollar for a real treasure, so with a minor investment you can haul home everything from state pamphlets on the feeding habits of bass in the delta to an old picture book of logging railroads.

If some special book you need is only available new, by all means get it at a museum shop. Their prices are rarely higher than a private bookstore, their selection often better and/or more specialized and your patronage helps them keep the museum open.

Again, always check for an index. Theoretically, writing the subject on the top of the page will help you retrieve information if there isn't an index, but generally it doesn't work.

I used to mark up all my books, writing in margins, noting subjects at the top of the page, making stars and such next to paragraphs I wanted to remember. I've found that in the long run it doesn't help that much, and it does destroy the value of the book, which you may someday wish to resell. Naturally if it's an old, dog-eared thing of no specific value, scribbling all over it won't hurt, but I think twice now before defacing a pristine (and sometimes expensive) new book.

To look at my bookcases, one would think I was obsessive on just one subject, for during any specific project I devote all my easy-to-get-to bookcases to the subject. Again, it's a question of retrieval; all the books on one aspect of my time and place are kept together. Thus the books on flora and fauna are in one case while those that deal with a particular culture are shelved together in another case. Oversized and art books are a problem and usually get stuck wherever they fit, while pamphlets and children's coloring books (which are often full of exactly what you need, visually) are propped up by similar subject hard copies. Magazine collections are all kept together, and I always get the index, if the publisher offers it.

Maps tend to be more unruly, stacking up so that you can't see the titles or sliding off shelves if you lay them flat, so I sometimes hang them, open and available, from one wall. And any form of artwork, whether it's a poster of wildflowers, tracks of wild animals or even a calendar picture that captures the feel of the land, gets displayed where I can see it readily.

Depending on how much you collect in the way of resource material, you may or may not need such a system. But if you do, take the time to work out an organization that is compatible with your needs . . . it will more than pay off in time saved when you get down to the act of actual writing.

(You may want to consider insuring your books separately, which will require making an inventory of titles and prices. This is a good time to organize your collection by subject as well, and if you alphabetize the list, you can take a copy with you to make sure you don't end up buying duplicates over a long period of time.)

SAVE ALL RECEIPTS

Yes, Virginia, the tax man cometh, and you need to be prepared to back up your professional costs if he wants to see proof.

In general authors can deduct all sorts of things that relate to creating a book; not only the cost of pens, paper, business calls, copying expenses and postage, but also computers and VCRs, magazine and newspaper subscriptions, cable TV, books and the space used exclusively for your work, including bookcases, map tables and any other oddments you require.

Since tax laws are fairly fluid, there may be various changes that apply specifically to authors. Writers' magazines occasionally publish articles about the tax laws and it's worth photocopying them for your CPA. She probably doesn't have too many clients in your profession, so good manners and enlightened self-interest suggest it's a good idea to provide her with whatever information you run across.

Among the two most important things to remember are (1) keep all receipts and (2) keep a written record of your travel expenses in a bound book—not one where pages can be removed or inserted.

This is true for any research trip, even if only of the one-day variety. There are a flurry of other details, for example, restaurant expenses are deductible up to a certain amount, providing the eatery is twenty-five miles from your home, but if the dinner tab is under a certain sum, no receipts are necessary, though you still get to record it in your expenses book. These are the kinds of things you can leave to your tax preparer once you've decided what you need to be concerned about and what not. Just as long as you remember to note your expenditures and save those receipts, the rest of your time and energy can be devoted to collecting the information you need.

Which brings up the question of researching on location. Is there any real value in actually traveling to the places you write about? Can you keep the cost within a reasonable amount? Are there specific advantages in on-site research? Is it worth the time and expense?

To all of which I respond with a rousing, "You bet, even if you have to live on macaroni and cheese for six months before you go!"

As mentioned earlier, a large part of being a historical novelist pays off not so much in money but in the perks of the lifestyle you can legitimately live. And one of those perks is traveling to your various locations—far or near, tame or exotic. Go ahead and plan for it . . . in the long run, it can only help your writing.

CHAPTER FIVE

You're Going Where?

F ew things are more confusing to a nonwriter than hearing that a hopeful novelist is heading for Timbuktu to do research. The very notion makes some people's hearts race with admiration and envy, while others curl up their toes in dismay, certain that it is a total waste of time and money.

Only the writer can decide whether such a trip is worthwhile. Some simply have no interest in going to their locations whereas others are willing to travel on the barest of shoestrings, without even a contract in their pockets, just to make certain they "get it right" in their books.

Research trips can be big or little—a day trip to a nearby city to see the Russian Circus was totally tax deductible for me as I had a dancing bear in the Guinevere book I was working on. Bears' knees bend in the opposite manner from ours (more like elbows than knees) and that's what makes them look so funny. But until I saw it, I had no idea what it was like. Although the trip itself was short, the information was worthwhile, so keep in mind that even little jaunts count if they provide what you need.

YES, BUT DO YOU REALLY NEED TO GO?

Bigger trips and longer stays are called for when the landscape itself plays a major part in the story. For instance, the Yorkshire moors are crucial to *Wuthering Heights* as they both shape and reflect the wild nature of the major characters in the story. The Brontë family lived on the edge of the moors, so Emily was quite familiar with them, seeing them as beautiful free places of exceptional solitude, yet brooding and violent as Heathcliff himself. That he should die chasing the phantom cries of Cathy's spirit carried on the long, lonesome wind is both fitting and specifically apt for the location—and was no doubt inspired by Emily's having listened to the mournful sound through many a long night.

It is not uncommon for a particular locale to invoke a whole scene in a book. It can be anything from something already planned to the kernel of a new direction you hadn't even thought of before. Certainly being able to stand or sit on the spot, and people the place with the characters of your mind can be wonderfully inspirational.

If the actual words start tapping on your consciousness, sit down and write them out, then and there if you possibly can. Sometimes a particular scene will spring to life, complete with minute detail, while other times it's more of the grand sweep and color, be it gray and misty or bright and sunny. Either way it's worth capturing on paper. You may or may not use the actual words you write in the final text, but usually there's an immediacy to them that will help reestablish the mood when you reread them back home. And occasionally a fine, stirring scene makes it from notebook scribble to finished text with no major changes.

If you don't happen to experience the living out of a scene on the spot, don't worry. You're still picking up lots and lots of information you couldn't get otherwise—the fall of light, the smell and direction of the wind, the sound (or lack) of nearby water. Remember that prior to the mid-1900s people were far more aware of and affected by these natural phenomena than we are today.

That was partly because they had no satellites and Doppler radar to show weather patterns, no instant news, no warning of what might be coming. They relied on sight, sound, smell or the ache in their rheumatic bones to forecast changes in weather. And a change in weather could mean disaster: "God willing and the creeks don't rise" was a folk saying my Connecticut grandmother used, and it clearly reflects how much at the mercy of the elements people were.

Blizzards might pile the snow into twenty-foot drifts. Mud slides, wildfires or ice storms meant isolation from the rest of the world; not only could you not get out, no one else could get in. If there wasn't enough food or a medical emergency arose, you were likely to die. So it behooved every one to be alert to signs of heavy weather since gauging whether it was safe to come, go or stay in one spot could mean the difference between life and death.

Then, too, geological features were not as easily overcome as they are nowadays. When we can span the continent in six hours, it's hard to remember it took six months just to cover two-thirds of it if you were hauling a wagon with all your possessions behind you. Rivers were major obstacles to be forded, swum, ferried across or bridged, depending on the size of the watercourse and your equipment.

Yet in spite of that, life in many antique or classical eras was far from primitive. Roman villas in the Britain of A.D. 350 had central heating, some form of indoor plumbing, elegant gardens, frescoes, mosaic floors and beautiful tableware. Winston Churchill himself noted that after the fall of Rome, it was another fourteen hundred years before the common man could live in the same kind of comfort and sanitation that the Romano-Briton took for granted.

Nor was it only the rich who enjoyed these benefits. Anyone could travel on the well-surveyed, graded and drained Roman roads that are often the basis of our modern highways in Europe and England today. It was common to cross flood plains on causeways and rivers on bridges whose footings were made of a waterproof cement that still survives in some Scottish rivers, and safety when traveling was assured by the legions keeping the verge of the road free of scrub and trees for as far back as an arrow's flight so that highwaymen had no place to lurk.

All of which points up the fact that we should never underestimate the past, either in its sophistication or its brutality. And always keep in mind that old admonition that every era is "modern" in the eyes of those who are living in it.

WHAT WOULD THEY HAVE SEEN?

For some of us, writing about an area we've never been to is not only chancy, it just doesn't work. I always feel as though my characters are floating about six inches above the floor if I've put them somewhere I haven't actually been. The present-day landscape may have changed somewhat—Who built that automobile factory in the middle of the jousting field?—but major geographical features don't change a lot from one century to another.

And if you don't go see for yourself, you may inadvertently overlook something that would have struck your earlier-living characters right between the eyes. For instance, outside of Gloucester the Cotswold escarpment rises up almost steeply enough to be called a cliff. It is amazing to look up at from the ground and breathtaking to look down from at the top. No one traveling between the Lake District and Winchester could miss it, whether going by horse or by foot. Yet while it was mentioned obliquely in various British geology books, it took actually being there and seeing it for the power to sink in. If I hadn't decided to make a second trip, specifically traveling the route my Gwen was taking, I would have missed it entirely. It turned out the old Roman Road she would have been on is too steep for modern public transportation, which is why I didn't see it the first time I was there—the bus took a different and far less dramatic route. Fortunately something prompted me to hire a taxi once I got to Cirencester, have the driver take me back down to Gloucester and then turn around and come back up the way Gwen's party would have. It was an extravagant expense but worth it in the long run, as the actual escarpment was so startling, to ignore it would be like leaving out the Atlantic Ocean in a book about Columbus discovering America.

The text of my first Guinevere book was being set in print, but I was able to add a page or two dealing with the trouble of climbing that escarpment and the amazing view from the top.

This approach may seem awfully nitpicky to some, but authenticity is one of the marks of my writing, and one goes on a research trip precisely to check out that sort of thing.

There are people who specialize in reconstructing what the world used to look like several centuries or even millennia ago by studying maps, geology and present-day scientific findings on everything from pollen samples to unrecorded earthquakes. Their work is most likely found in books, and often in the locales about which they write, so keep your eyes open for these books wherever you go.

BEFORE YOU LEAVE

Realizing when you are roughly a quarter of the world away that you overlooked something really important is asking for serious frustration. The best way to avoid this is to start making a list of goals—places to go, things to see, people to talk to, ideas to check out, maps to get, etc.—as soon as you start thinking of taking a major research trip. Keep your list somewhere special (the back of my notebook, on the refrigerator or next to the computer work for me), and jot down whatever comes up as your academic research progresses.

Then as your trip begins to take shape timewise, financially and mentally, you'll have a nucleus of places to go and things to see. Much of your itinerary will depend on what's on your list—museums, celebrations, special events, conferences and conventions that you've noted over the last year or so. By all means write to museum curators, newspaper editors and librarians telling them you're coming and why and asking if they can recommend people to answer specific questions. Often you'll get a response complete with name and address of a local scholar who knows about the building of bows, the habits of wild sheep or whatever else fits in with your original query. From there it's only one more letter to that person explaining why you're coming to her part of the world and inquiring whether you might meet with her while you are there. Most people like to talk about what they know about, and if you make sure to write well ahead of time, you may find a cordial welcome from the president of the local Garden Society who specializes in native plants or the curator of antiquities at the nearby museum. If you have both money and space, offer some appropriate memento from the States when you meet—an American herbal calendar, for instance—remember to write your thank-you notes promptly.

Always allow plenty of time for side trips, as you're likely to run into more things there in a week than you can list in a month of research back home.

Naturally some things end up being closed, concluded, rained out, moved on or cancelled, so you can't adhere absolutely to such a list, but knowing what all you'd like to cover on any particular trip goes a long way toward helping you get—and stay—organized.

WHEN TO GO

Most hopeful or struggling authors can't afford to go trotting off to South America, Europe or around the Pacific Rim whenever the whim takes them. Nor can they stay for a prolonged time, usually. So it's wise to have a good idea both of your goals—locations and events you can't miss—and how you're going to get there.

First off, if you've never been to your chosen country before, get yourself a good guide book and map with railroads and rivers, highways and towns on it. You'll find it useful in writing the actual book and an absolute necessity for planning your trip.

It's easy to glance at a small map, see where you want to go and assume that bus, train or car will take you there. But there may be an intervening mountain range, a lack of rails or simply no roads cutting across that way, so what is only a hundred miles as the crow flies may require a circuitous route that takes all day by road or rail.

While bus schedules are often a mystery even to locals, most countries make their train schedules available to travel agents and prospective visitors who write and request them. Once you know where you want to go, that's a good place to start. If you simply can't get the information, find a more detailed map and check out rails, roads and ferry routes for yourself before deciding whether to buy a rail pass or not. (These are generally cheaper when purchased in the States, but you may find that trains go too fast. More about that later.) If it's not possible to plot your transportation, you may just have to wait and see what's available once you get there.

The airfares to other countries are generally subject to seasonal change, that is, higher in the most popular time (usually summer) and lower during the off-season or winter months. Naturally you'd rather avoid the mobs of vacationers but not have to slog around in the snow and sleet of a northern winter. That's where the "shoulder" fares come in. They extend from one to two months in spring and fall, put you in your destination when the bulk of the tourists have gone home and cost less than high-season tickets.

(Don't forget, if you are crossing the equator, you'll be changing seasons—our summer months are, in Rio, the middle of winter. Even if you're not headed for such exotic locales, be sure to check the kind of weather and what is recommended by way of clothes; in summer the Lake District of England can have capricious weather, and in the tropics you expect it to rain most every day.)

Many hotels and bed-and-breakfasts also have seasonal rates, but some museums and historically reconstructed theme parks are closed during winter, so you'd be wise to make sure just how long they stay open. There are a few things more discouraging than going all the way out to Hamlet's castle only to find it was shut down last week. By all means write, ask your travel agent or check the Net for schedules at your most important destinations.

Another advantage of shoulder travel is that the weather is usually milder in spring and fall. If you go in May, you can look forward to warming as June approaches, but being chilly in September means you should plan to buy a nice warm jacket if you're going to stay on into October. This gives you a chance to pick up clothes that would be prohibitively expensive here in the States; Scottish woolens or cashmeres, for instance. Check your library for the U.S. Customs pamphlets on what you can bring in from abroad; as I recall some things, if worn regularly, are seen as necessities, not luxuries, and don't have to be declared.

MAKING IT PAY

If you're traveling on a tight budget, consider possible spin-off articles for papers or magazines to help the trip pay for itself. There are all sorts of publications that could be interested in a story about your destination: airline and travel magazines, retirement magazines and supplements, local newspapers that can't afford a travel editor but might be interested in something with a special slant their direction and, of course, specialty publications.

Say, for instance, you're going to an area such as Cheddar Gorge, which is renowned for its cheese. You could write up a history of that product and see about marketing it to papers in the dairy and cheese areas of the States. Or contact the Dairy Industry ahead of time. Chances are they have a trade publication and will let you know what articles they're specifically interested in: "We did one on Cheddar last year, but if you get to Wales, check out Caerphilly; maybe do an article that compares it with our own Philadelphia cream cheese."

There are any number of ways to spin off articles about what you see and find to help defray your expenses, so keep an open mind and eyes.

PACKING UP

As the time approaches you'll need to consider what to take and how to pack. Because you'll be moving from place to place in your research, I suggest limiting your luggage to one soft-sided suitcase or backpack (mine doubles as either) and one camera bag, sans camera. If you're a dedicated photographer your camera will be an invaluable tool, but if you're only a casual shutterbug, you'll find it cheaper and easier to buy postcards and slides of those things you want a visual record of. By doing so you get only the shots you really want and avoid the cost of film and camera insurance, as well as the extra weight and worry of the camera itself. By all means consider that an option, unless having a picture of yourself standing next to a historical monument is absolutely necessary for your own well-being.

If you leave your camera at home, you'll find your camera bag a wonderful day pack. Camera bags are usually divided into several sections for ease of organization and are big enough for notebook, pens, soap and other toiletries, plus an apple or bag of fruit from the local grocer when you go on a hike up the trail behind the castle ruins.

With only these two pieces of luggage, plus a belt purse for money, passport and such, your hands are free, you don't need to wait at the baggage claim, and you'll be able to move easily from place to place without having to hire taxis and bellboys unless you want to.

Over and above my usual pants and shirts I once took two dresses, a pair of dress shoes and even a large English umbrella of the kind called a "brawly." The brawly kept tripping me and poking others on buses or subways, so I turned it in to the man at the Lost and Found when I reached Victoria Station, figuring he'd find a home for it with someone who needed and wanted it more than I did.

The dress clothes were worn once (when I had tea with a lord who was a specialist in northern English forests), then sent home via surface mail. And the dress shoes were an aberration never again repeated. Ever since then I've placed usefulness above vanity and have been far more comfortable. It's nice to dress up now and then, but a research trip is not the time for it, and with the casualness of today's culture, I have no qualms about going to the opera in tennis shoes *if* I really want to take in the opera.

It's amazing how little you can get by with. I lived for six weeks in two pair of pants (in cooler climes the old-fashioned Navy sailor pants from the surplus stores are great as they are wool, washable and practically indestructible), two shirts, one of which should be drip-dry, and several T-shirts (both because they keep you warmer as the weather cools and they keep your shirts fresher longer). Underwear, a couple of different weight and style sweaters and a warm parka give you just about everything else you need. If you're going to a rainy place, Scotland or the tropic, for instance, I suggest some form of lightweight weatherproof coat or cape; even disposable plastic ones work, and they don't take up much space in your bag. Things like scarves or caps for keeping your head and ears warm can be picked up at your destination; not only will you find a selection that is geared specifically to the climate, you'll bring home a memento to enjoy for years to come.

THE TOOLS OF YOUR CRAFT

There are any number of techniques for capturing research information, from tape recorders to commercial videos, slides to postcards. But no matter what else gets taken or left behind, it's a rare author who doesn't carry a notebook. Maybe it's because we express ourselves best with the written word or just because notebooks are inexpensive and easy to operate. If you're on a research trip, your best bet will be a bound notebook into which you can scribble notes, addresses, points and ideas (P&I) and expenses.

The usual spiral kind works just fine and is easy to get. I find the 9½" × 6" is the best size for me, fitting into a large purse, small day pack or camera bag, but the 8½" × 11" would do as well if you can carry it easily.

Always put your name, address and phone number on the first page, using a big marker and heavy letters. I write *REWARD* and *PLEASE RETURN TO* as well; my notebook's only been lost once, and it was sent back after someone picked it up in San Francisco, which wouldn't have happened if there hadn't been an identifying sheet in the front.

The reward needn't be large, but when you stop to think how many months of research, information and addresses could have been lost forever, you'll see how worthwhile it is. Also be sure you add whatever postage the returner had to buy to get it back to you. It's not only good manners; she may watch for your book to come out and feel a certain pride of involvement.

I buy different colored notebooks and write the working title of the novel plus the year on the cover so that it's easily recognizable. Believe me, after a decade you can have quite a collection of the things.

The ones I get are divided into five or six sections and at first I tried to use the different sections for different things: travel plans up front, museum visits and archaeological discoveries in the middle, a P&I section of its own and an entry for every penny spent beginning at the last page of the last section and working forward— there's nothing that says you have to use a book from front to back only, after all, and knowing exactly where the money page is can be a help.

Over the years, however, I've found that I'm more likely to remember something not by subject but by the when and where I found it on my trip, so most of those artificial divisions just get confusing. Now I note whatever comes up as it comes up, whether it's about the use of elder twigs to make flutes (the center is hollow) or the name of the president of the Pony Express Society in California, and am usually able to retrieve the materials with much less confusion. Don't forget to date every page, and note what trip or location is involved. (This, along with the date and amount of money spent on gas, food or lodging, helps to verify your deduction if the IRS ever audits you.)

The two exceptions to the above are a separate section for jotting down P&Is as they come to you and the money pages at the back of the book. This is also the place to list *all* books and pamphlets bought, the amount paid and when they were mailed home if you don't take them with you. (More on that in the next chapter.)

ALONE OR WITH A COMPANION?

This is probably the single most confusing decision you'll need to make about research trips, whether domestic or foreign. Part of it depends on who is available when you need to go, and part is where you want to go. Because the language barrier is minimal and our cultures are so similar, I have no qualms about traveling alone in Britain, Canada, New Zealand or Australia, but would definitely hold off going to Greece or Turkey until I could find a companion who knows his way around—or even join a group tour, if necessary.

But over and above those considerations is the question of compatibility. It's wonderfully helpful to have someone else drive the car while you take notes, help you pack up the books to mail home and arrange for the next night's lodging while you're studying the map and deciding whether to go on the nature walk you read about in the local paper.

Naturally there will be times and places when compromise with your traveling companion is easy; she can go shopping, to a movie or exploring the modern art galleries while you are looking up things in the archives of the local library. But if conflicts arise it's hard to concentrate on research when your companion is sulking, bored or outright demanding that you pay attention to her needs for a change.

Then, too, even the best of traveling companions can pose a problem if he wants to talk about his own thoughts while you're trying to organize yours. This is one of the biggest and least expected of difficulties and can only be dealt with by trial and error. One person is sensitive enough to see that you're frowning over your notebook and he will leave you alone, while another is bubbling over with his own reactions or discoveries and hasn't a clue to the fact that he's driving you crazy. Nor, in all fairness, should you expect everyone else to understand what's happening in your head or to adjust *all* his time and plans to your needs.

So selecting a traveling companion comes down to how well do you know the person, how comfortable have you been on day trips together, how compatible are your tastes, interests, financial arrangements and expectations about this trip?

Is she comfortable with the fact that this is a business trip for you? Are there areas of expertise or interest on her part that will provide you with new information and make her feel important and involved? (A geologist, botanist or wild-animal specialist can be a marvelous companion if she will share her observations and you have sense enough to appreciate them.)

All in all, the question of whether to go alone or with a companion is just as individual as the decision to take such a trip to begin with. Only you know how important it is to you and can gauge whether it will be truly helpful. No matter how much fun research trips can be, the fact remains that they're only successful if they add depth to your book and strength to your characters.

◆ ◆ ◆

There are, of course, many other things you could take with you, but these bare-bones supplies should both get you by and give you enough confidence to take off, either on your own or with a companion, for what could tun out to be the trip of a lifetime.

CHAPTER SIX

While You're There

One of the delights of a research trip is the fact that you can stand and gawk at anything that captures your interest, ask all sorts of questions, get behind all kinds of scenes, meet all sorts of people. If you're like me, you'll be absorbing everything you can about this new landscape, so it's just as well to have things such as lodgings fairly well in hand before you go wandering off across the countryside.

WHERE TO STAY

As in this country, the cost of lodging ranges from horrifically expensive to downright cheap, depending on location, amenities and time of year. Since most authors can't afford the Ritz but would rather not stay in a flophouse, finding reasonable accommodations, either here or overseas, can be a real challenge.

Youth Hostels

These are a wonderful solution if you're even mildly adventurous. They are usually the cheapest safe and clean accommodations; allow you to cook your own breakfast and dinner, thereby saving restaurant costs; are conveniently located and generally full of interesting people.

The British hostels are located a day's walk apart, often in the most beautiful areas, and may be found in buildings ranging from a fifteenth-century mill, complete with millrace right outside the bathroom window, to a country estate, an unused church or a cathedral dormitory. They are open to anyone of any age, and you're likely to meet everyone from an octogenarian poetess who spends her summer moseying about the English countryside to whole families of parents, children and grandchildren enjoying an outing together. (Some other countries limit the use to people under thirty years old, so you'd best check before you go.)

Also at hostels you'll probably encounter someone who has just come from where you are heading, so you can exchange road information, train or bus schedules and tips about out-of-the-way places you might otherwise have missed.

Since hostels were originally set up for young travelers (hikers and such), who only needed a roof at night and a place to gather and exchange information around a fire, most are only open at night—generally from 5 P.M. to 9 A.M.—and are closed throughout the day. Accommodations are simple and sleeping arrangements are often dormitory style, usually with bunk beds. You'll be expected to do whatever small chore the warden gives you each morning, and will need to bring your own towel, soap, food and bed sheet (a lightweight sack that you take with you from place to place, thereby doing away with the need for washing linens). Blankets, comforters and even pillows are provided by the hostel.

All but the most primitive have communal kitchens well supplied with pots, pans, cups and plates, though in Scotland you are expected to have your own silverware. And no matter where you are, you'll need to supply your own matches for lighting the gas burners.

Most hostels have a small stock of food for sale: fresh milk, butter, eggs, canned meats and various sundries such as soap, toothpaste or postcards. Many provide a hot meal both in the evening and for breakfast if you put your name in ahead of time. The quality of cooking varies from warden to warden, but if you're cold and tired at the end of the day, anything looks good. Naturally, whether you cook your own or eat with the warden, you're expected to wash your dishes and help keep the kitchen clean.

I generally eat my main meal at lunch while I'm out and about; in Britain pub lunches of steak and kidney pie or fish and chips can be wonderful. Then toward evening I pick up a head of lettuce or other veggies, some bread, fruit and a dessert on the way to the hostel. Once settled in I get tea bags, a bottle of milk and two fresh eggs or cheese for breakfast from the warden, all of which I eat before leaving the hostel for the next day's adventure. That way I'm not carrying food around with me but manage a fairly balanced diet on a pittance.

While the fancier hostels have washing machines and driers, the rest have at least a set-tub and drying room. If you take your shower when you first get there in the evening, your towel will be dry when you pack up to move on come morning. If you're staying over another night, you can leave your pack there, being sure to take with you anything you'll need during the day as the hostel will be closed until evening.

In Britain there is a three-night limit to keep people from moving into hostels for prolonged stays. In recent years, however, some hostels have developed family accommodations as well as the traditional dormitory arrangements so that couples and families with children can be together. The rules may be somewhat different for these places, and if you're interested, ask about them when you get your information from the International Hostel Association office nearest you.

If you become a member you will receive an updated book with the particulars for each hostel and all the information for booking in advance. By all means read the book; many popular hostels require reservations, and the book will tell you when and how to make them. (I generally go down the middle between winging it and having it all planned out and reserved weeks ahead of time. If you call your next hostel destination before 9 A.M., you can usually book lodging for that night, which leaves you free to decide where to go on a daily basis but assures you a roof once you've charted your course. You do, however, have to be willing to look elsewhere if all the hostels in the area are full at such late notice.)

Bed-and-Breakfasts

The next most reasonable accommodations are bed-and-breakfasts (B&Bs). Although such places are very pricey here in the States, in Europe they are much less pretentious, being simply a back bedroom put up for rent on a nightly basis by any working class family. Many are inexpensive, and sometimes you end up staying on a farm where you can feed the chickens or help milk the cow if you wish.

The cheaper B&Bs in city or town are usually near the train or bus stops and are therefore easy to get to. Most are simply walk-in—a vacancy sign will be in the window or door—but if you find one you really enjoy, by all means take their card and contact them about staying there next time you're in the area. As one author said, there's nothing like a friendly welcome from someone who remembers you to make the end of a grueling day more pleasant.

In the more rural parts of Britain you'll sometimes find a sixteenth- or seventeenth-century cottage inhabited by a retired couple, who make a few extra pounds by letting out the grandchildren's room during travel season. Again, it's personable, pleasant and far less expensive than a city hotel would be.

Planning Ahead

Advance planning is always a good idea, whether you're staying at a series of hostels, B&Bs or hotels. Booking ahead is a good idea in the most popular areas or times. Don't forget that other countries have different vacation days, Bank Holiday in Britain being a case in point. Just as you wouldn't want to be a traveler without a reservation during Memorial or Labor Days here, it's wise to plan out and verify your lodging during national holidays in a foreign country.

By the same token, different areas have different banking hours or local customs. Once in Scotland I put off stopping at an open bank in one town, figuring that I'd change my traveler's check in the next town when I stopped for lunch. But the next town was in a different county, and all the banks had the day off. The same thing can happen with drugstores (many rural areas have never heard of stores staying open in the evening) or even food stores, so my general rule of thumb is BUY IT WHEN YOU FIND IT. If the store's open here and now, get whatever you need or risk having to do without.

ON LOCATION

No matter how comprehensive you've tried to be beforehand, being on the site is going to bring up all sorts of new ideas and discoveries. For instance, there are many little museums no one mentions in the travel books. So while you're there, make a point of checking out all the museums you can. They will often give you tremendous insight into local problems—and solutions—or antique customs. For instance, at the Kendal Museum in the heart of England's wool district, one discovers that in the really old days they didn't shear sheep but just walked through the land literally gathering the wool off the bushes where the sheep had stopped to scratch, much as the American Indians still pluck the soft under-wool of the buffalo from bushes and shrubs. Though the Romans developed a handy type of scissor to do the job on sheep, as far as I know no one has ever tried to shear a buffalo. (This is, obviously, the origin of our term "woolgathering," as well as a nice bit of color that helps sustain your fictional world.)

Museum members are usually very helpful, particularly if they're in an out-of-the-way village. I actually held a fifteen-hundred-year-old lamp in my hand, thanks to a marvelous little lady in Millom who opened the museum for me when she saw me standing, disconsolate, in front of the sign saying "Closed 'til Whitsun." She was so charmed to hear that I'd come all the way from California to see her museum after reading about it in one of the Nicholson's guides to England, she immediately ran home and got the key to let me in.

Sometimes new authors are afraid to mention what they're working on, for fear someone else will steal their ideas. Fiction is so personal, however, it's hard to imagine two identical novels, so I'd say by all means tell the museum people what you're researching; often it will lead the locals to volunteer information you'd never run across otherwise.

One of the major reasons for a research trip is to collect books and pamphlets that are not available in this country. *Beekeeping Secrets in the North* or *The Red Deer of Lakeland* can be invaluable once you get back home, even though they're only pamphlets or children's books from the ranger's station. Children's books are often the best help, by the way. They have clear and easily understood information, usually with lots of pictures, and are far less expensive than whole volumes on the same subject.

Always watch for books and pamphlets on the native flora and fauna. Believe me, when you need to know what blooms outside of Glastonbury in April, you don't want to wait for correspondence with the Glastonbury Garden Club, who might or might not understand that you're looking for wild plants only, not recent introductions. It will be worth the cost to have a pamphlet, preferably with pictures, at your disposal once you get home.

Remember that bookstores will focus on different things in different areas, and there's a chance you'll find the biography of a person in one locale but not another. I was looking for information on Ned Baker, an Illinois attorney and friend of Abraham Lincoln's who came to California during the gold rush. Although there are both streets and forts named for him, the only biography listed in the California libraries is a local author's efforts from a decade back. That book was out of print and appeared to be both rare and expensive.

Then I went browsing in a used-book store while on a family visit to Oregon and guess what? The town of Baker, Oregon, was named for my man, and the Oregon Historical Society had published a comprehensive biography because he was Oregon's first senator. His entire stay in California was covered by the Oregon book, and since they had five copies in the store, I got it for a very reasonable price.

So keep your eyes open on the one hand, and remember that there may be some other, less obvious tie-in you can use to track these things down.

THE JOY OF REENACTMENTS

There's nothing like spending half an hour jouncing along in a covered wagon, watching the rise and fall of the draft animal rumps in front of you, to bring home why most pioneer women *walked* the length of the Emigrant Trail. Not only did the animals need to have as light a load as possible, the women's stomachs would have had to be made of cast iron to survive all that pitching and swaying.

No matter what era you're researching, you most likely will find someone, somewhere has set up some kind of reenactment, whether it's Williamsburg in the 1700s, Civil War sites in the South or various uprisings, rebellions and triumphs throughout the rest of the world.

In Europe you'll find all manner of local celebrations. If England's Pitchfork Rebellion is your style, write to the tourism center, or the chamber of commerce of the major towns involved, asking if there are pageants or festivals you can come to. They'll be thrilled to know someone across the sea is interested and no doubt send you back not only calendars but also a list of B&Bs, hotels and historical associations you can contact.

Also, look for various theme parks of an educational nature. At Queen Elizabeth II Park in England there's a complete reconstruction of a Celtic roundhouse where archaeologists live in the old manner, thereby rediscovering all sorts of things our great great ancestors knew but we have since forgotten. Since these places are designed to be learning centers, the staff is usually delighted to hear from people wanting to know more. Often you'll have a chance to take part in the activities, whether at a Danish Dark Age village or an Irish medieval feast.

In the United States you'll find the Renaissance Fair, the Mountain Men Rendezvous, Pony Express celebrations, various covered wagon journeys and in the southwest, Mexican and Indian festivities as well. So write to the chambers of commerce, tourism centers and local newspapers to determine what's happening.

Hands-on experience is always best for good reason; the physical, visceral response is often different from what the mind conjures on its own. But if you yourself can't participate in an activity, by all means interview people who have. Ask what they noticed most, what they liked most, what they liked least and how they would describe it, etc. There are hundreds of things, from the softness of one's skin after working with unwashed fleece to the way a goat steps sideways if you try to milk her with cold hands, that will add reality for your reader and strengthen the credibility of the world you're creating.

PAYING THE PIPER

I prefer to carry traveler's checks, though I also take along the single credit card that I use for nothing but deductible expenses. By keeping all tax deductibles on the one card, I let the plastic company do my bookkeeping for me when it comes time to separate out what's professional expense and what's personal.

One of the advantages of credit card purchases in other countries lies in the time it takes to get the bills processed; sometimes it's a month or more before they come through, which gives you time to get home before you have to pay for them. The disadvantage is that the exchange rate may change against you during that time and leave you paying more in dollars than you intended. But in general I've never had any trouble in getting either MasterCard or Visa accepted, and it's nice to know there's a cushion there if you need it while traveling far from home.

If you're truly single-minded and only spend your money on things that are somehow related to your book, you can deduct all expenses for the entire research trip. That includes *everything* even food at the tavern where you chat with the owner about local customs, estates and legends. Taking a boat trip down the Rhine, attending a hunting dog trial in the English Lakes or going to a medieval dinner festival put on in the Borders are all professionally useful as long as they specifically relate to the locale, activity or history in your fiction. You can deduct such expenses from your taxes during the year they were incurred even if you don't see any financial return from them for several more years. (Naturally there's nothing to keep you from spending money on unrelated sidetrips; they just won't be among the costs you can deduct.)

And, of course, it would be difficult to explain how a trip to and stay at one of Las Vegas's major casinos was a professional expense if your subject is a medieval French nun, not *The Godfather.*

The same goes for items purchased. Photos, curios and examples of folk art (such as carved wooden figures) can be considered either examples of local crafts and culture or necessary for your ambiance at home. On the other hand, buying an authentic (and therefore pricey) etching probably wouldn't pass muster with the IRS, even if the artist was the subject of your novel, just as the purchase of a gold and garnet necklace wouldn't qualify simply because the Saxons were so fond of that combination in jewelry. In both these cases, reproductions would no doubt do just as well for your research and be far less aggravating to the tax people.

GETTING AROUND

Traveling in another country is always an adventure. Even here at home it's impossible to drive and take notes at the same time, and if you're also trying to negotiate driving on what seems like the wrong side of the road, it's well-nigh impossible. Therefore I strongly suggest looking at your other options.

Buses

Buses are often the best for local trips—trains go so fast you can't see more than the overall landscape and planes are usually up too high to count. Try to sit up front where you'll have the broadest view; it's tempting to sit on the top story if there is one, but remember your characters would either be riding or walking along at ground level and not see the same things you're seeing from up there.

Sometimes a seatmate will prove talkative. A friendly charwoman riding home from her work in Carlisle one evening told me all about Border architecture: houses built so the cows could be driven into the ground floor while the people climbed to the upper stories when the raiders swooped down from Scotland. Also, local bus drivers can be most helpful. If you're going to be staying in one area for several days or a week, get a local bus pass and just ride around, looking at *everything* and taking all sorts of notes. Chances are, if you're sitting up near the driver, he'll ask what you're doing and might well have tips about locally known places, legends and haunts that will add color to your work.

Taxicabs

Cabs are certainly expensive if your budget is tight, but indispensable if you need to go to out-of-the-way places and usually better than going home without seeing all that you came for, and may need to know. If you're lucky, the cabby will be interested as well, particularly if you explain where you need to go, how long you expect to be there and determine a set price with her beforehand. That way you can poke around the ruins, the library or forest as much as you need to because everyone has already agreed upon the time and money involved.

Rental Cars

If you know where you're going and how to get there, rental cars are another possibility. I did it during four of my five Guinevere trips to Britain and never had an accident, in spite of the English driving on the right-hand side of the road. If you decide to do the same, I suggest renting your car on a Friday afternoon in a semi-rural town so you can practice your driving over the whole weekend, when traffic is more sporadic. By Monday rush hour you'll probably even be able to negotiate roundabouts with real confidence.

In countries where there is none of the confusion of driving on the "wrong" side of the road, you may not even need the weekend to adapt, though city driving anywhere is likely to have hazards peculiar to itself.

Additionally, each country has its own pattern of travel. Buses are generally cheap and (with luck) will reach just about everywhere. But if it is more than a local trip, you may have to go way out of your way to get there, much as U.S. airlines have you fly through their hub terminals. In England, Birmingham is one such center: every bus line arrives by 2:30 P.M., and there's a mad scramble while travelers exchange buses in the huge barn where the vehicles are lined up six to eight deep and six to eight across. At 3:00 sharp they are all revved up and ready to wheel out into the streets of the city, each one off and running for its new destination.

Considering that the whole of Britain fits pretty much in the state of California, that may be the most sensible way of doing it, but it makes you go to Birmingham whether it's on your way or not, and the trip may require the better part of a day rather than just a couple of hours. So unless you've already been to your destination before and know for certain when and how things run, it's wise to stay fairly flexible on timing, and find out how long it's going to take to get from here to there if you do have a reservation or other commitment to keep.

MAILING THINGS HOME

Books not only weigh a lot, they take up lots of space, either in your luggage or your arms. So it is not illogical to mail them home, usually in small batches as your trip progresses. Since they'll be going by other transport sooner or later, why cart them around? On my first sojourn to Britain, I cleverly packed up all my clothes and shipped them home the day before flying back in order to fill my backpack with books. It's a grand idea you'll never do more than once because books weigh a ton, and if you can barely drag yourself and your boodle to the tag end of the customs line, you'll have defeated the whole idea of taking nothing but carry-on luggage. So although it can add as much as 30 to 50 percent to the price of the books, it's well worth it to mail them home "airmail insured."

Normally you can buy good sturdy boxes at the post offices in Britain and Europe, though you'll probably need to carry a roll of wide plastic tape and a small pair of scissors or pocket knife with which to cut it.

As you pack each box, make a special and specific inventory list on a separate page in your notebook, beginning with the location and date the box was sent. This list needs to include title, author, publisher and price. On that same page note the amount of postage for that particular box, the cost and amount of insurance and the voucher number if there is one. That way you'll have all the information together for tax purposes, and if one of your boxes is lost, you'll have the information to file for the insurance.

I've only lost two boxes in transit. One was in surface mail, uninsured, which meant there was no real way to trace it, and it never did show up. The second was insured, thank goodness, as it proved to be a major problem, and an excellent example of why using a credit card for research materials is a good idea. I'd bought several hundred dollars worth of books and maps at a sizeable bookstore that offered to pack and send the books home for me. When the box hadn't arrived after a month, I called the store to track it down. The staff there claimed to have sent it, but after six weeks I challenged the charge on my credit card, and we discovered it had not gone by airmail as promised and may or may not have been insured. Since I'd paid them both an insurance and postage fee and the goods never arrived, all charges were removed from my credit card. (Most credit card customer relations departments are really helpful if a store doesn't meet its responsibility, and because of the time lag in billing, you'll be sure that the goods are delivered intact before you have to pay for them.)

While the cost and trouble of "airmail insured" may seem exorbitant to some, surface mail, even from Britain, is not only slow but somewhat unreliable. Airmail sometimes gets your books home before you; at the most there shouldn't be more than a week or two delay, which is far better than waiting for a package that never comes. I know another author who fretted for eight months over a package that was to take a month from London, surface mail. As he hadn't insured it, he had no recourse except to grumble about the great maps and good books he'd paid for but doesn't have, and last time I saw him he specifically noted he'd *never* do that again.

Another advantage of sending things home airmail lies in the fact that when you get home yourself, chances are your head will be full of all sorts of new ideas and directions, colors and characters. Having your new material right there and handy can be a grand incentive to get started writing as soon as you get over the jet lag. After all, that magnum opus won't wait forever!

PART TWO

Work In Progress

Rousing Story, Engaging People

O nce you know what kind of book you want to write and you're feeling fairly comfortable with your era, it's time to go back and refine the story and people that got you started on all this research to begin with. What have you learned that will change or enhance your story? Are there specific historic events that can be used to show your characters' makeup? How can they be worked into the story? And do the characters and plot still ring as true as you originally thought?

Although plot and character development are different components of a novel, each grows out of the other: You need a plot that allows your characters to develop in certain ways, and you need characters that keep the drama of your plot going. This is true of any novel, but in historical fiction you have the added dimension of playing off the historical setting as well.

For instance, Morton Thompson's book *Not As a Stranger*, deals with a turn-of-the century lad who's fascinated by the horse-and-buggy doctors of his childhood and yearns to become a physician himself. He manages, by hook or crook, to get through college and into medical school, only to discover his improvident father has taken *all* the money that was to pay for school and invested it in a harness-making business. The father shrugs off the newfangled machines called automobiles as simply a flash in the pan, but the reader follows the story with sinking heart, knowing the father's action is going to render his son's dream impossible.

Since the threat to the boy's schooling is crucial to the plot, this is, like *The Scarlet Letter*, a masterful weaving together of social history, plot and character conflicts. Thompson could have had the father lose the money some other way, say, by gambling. But that would hardly have the irony this choice does . . . and since the money had to be lost, it's stronger to play it out in a way that evokes the essence of the era as well.

The evolution of plot is, in and of itself, a broad, complex and exciting subject. Since I'm focusing primarily the use of history in fiction, my examples will deal largely with how to weave historical reality into your plot, rather than exploring the subject of plotting by itself. However, there are a number of excellent books written about plotting that I'm glad to recommend.

First off is Ansen Dibell's *Plot*. This is one of the best books I've encountered; Dibell covers everything from overall construction to the importance of opening scenes; looks at pacing, exposition, transitions and contrasts, juxtaposition, techniques and conclusions—all with a keen wit as well as a clear style. Any writer, whether novice or master, can learn from this work, and I strongly recommend it, no matter where you are in your career.

Dean Koontz also wrote a small volume entitled *How to Write Best-Selling Fiction*, which is right on with its advice. And William Noble is renowned for his books on crafting novels, most of which are still in print and definitely worth learning from. They each deal with slightly different aspects of the subject, so what you miss in one's approach, you find in another's.

Remember that most any story can fit into any era, as human nature doesn't change that much from one epoch to another. But no matter how interesting you make the world around your characters, if you don't have a strong plot that makes the most of your chosen time frame, no one will care.

THE IMPORTANCE OF CONFLICT

As William Noble points out, conflict is the essence of drama, and drama is what novels are all about. Without conflict your characters have no story; they are simply part of a tableau that may create mood but doesn't move. To be interesting and entertaining, your book has to be about people striving for something while other people or circumstances keep them from achieving it, thereby introducing *conflict*. Not all such struggles are full of blood and violence, but they are rich in drama. The reader wants to sweat and struggle with the characters, and share the results whether that be tears or triumph.

Classically, conflict falls into five specific categories; man against himself, man against man, man against society, man against nature and man against God.

For instance, *The Red Badge of Courage* deals with man against himself, as the protagonist spends most of the book trying to find a way to live with himself after he's committed what he considers to be an act of cowardice.

Shaara's *The Killer Angels* hinges on the conflict of man against man, exploring as it does the differences in temperament, philosophy and motivations of the opponents at Gettysburg, most of them in middle command and some at odds with their own commanders.

Dickens's *A Tale of Two Cities* studies people in conflict with their society, from the downtrodden masses who liberate the Bastille to the innocent aristocrats who fall victim to the ensuing Reign of Terror.

Laura Ingalls Wilder's *Little House on the Prairie,* while not dealing with specific historical events, certainly captures a bygone era when frontier people struggled constantly against nature just to stay alive.

And Melville's *Moby Dick* is, in its way, a mixture of man against nature and man against God, as Ahab's obsession with the great whale verges on battling both the sacred and profane.

It's important to keep these themes in mind, and every so often while you're constructing your plot and characters, stop to ask who represents which conflict in your story. It can be a single focus, as in *The Red Badge of Courage,* or a multilevel saga, as in Tolstoy's *War and Peace,* where different people are in conflict over different things for different reasons.

It can also be as subjective as Scarlett trying to capture Ashley Wilkes's heart and commitment or as objective as Renault's *The Mask of Apollo,* which traces the downfall of democracy in Athens during the years right after Socrates' death, as seen by an actor who is one step removed from the historical characters.

All of the above are studies of conflict, and each is presented in a way that makes the reader care about the outcome, which is generally the difference between an enthusiastic response by readers and a lukewarm one. Just as you should be aware of the historical events during your era in order to decide which to use and how, so you'll write a more entertaining book if you keep the characters' conflicts in mind and make sure they build appropriately.

LAYING OUT THE PLOT

The long, leisurely book that includes lots of descriptive or philosophical narrative is clearly a thing of the past—action is what sells, and therefore that's what publishers buy. So now's the time to look at the arc of your story and see where the action lies—what discovery, confrontation, realization or surprise twist comes when. These are what Dibell calls "set pieces": big scenes that you build up to, that change something major in your characters' world and leave the reader feeling entertained, fulfilled and curious as to how this event will affect everyone else.

Sometimes such scenes are generated purely by the characters, as when Anna Karenina, despairing of her life either with or without her lover, throws herself under the wheels of the juggernaut train. I personally prefer to have actual historical events trigger such scenes whenever possible and therefore used the records of historic Saxon treachery in Britain to set up why Arthur refuses to trust the Saxons or his own son, whom he sent to be an ambassador to them. It is this distrust that actually triggers the final, desperate battle between father and son.

But whether your drama is history or character driven, the story needs to keep moving, so start building the arc of your book by looking at what elements offer the most drama, or else arrange your story to connect it with the most dramatic historical moments. At this stage you should still be flexible enough to incorporate either or both of these philosophies.

WHEN THE STORY IS IN PLACE

If you're working on a biography or a legend, the story line is already set to a large degree. So the first thing for you to consider is what you can bring to it that is new, relevant or intriguing because all publishers will ask, "Why should I put up the money to print your version when someone else's is already available?"

Often the answer has to do with a new point of view, historical perspective or the desire to reassess a well-known sacred cow. For instance, someone ought to retell *Cinderella* in a way that doesn't stress the lucky girl going from rags-to-riches, but rather the fact that the prince was willing to have everyone, even a scullery maid, try on the shoe. It was his perceptiveness, not just her good fortune, which was the original point of the story, after all.

Another fresh approach may be in how you envision your characters rather than a new perspective on the matter itself. You keep the traditional story but work backward on the character development, searching for clues as to *why* the people involved did what they did. What flaws or strengths inherent in their makeups explain their actions? How would these things show up in their childhoods? Teen years? Adult lives? What can you focus on, either already in the story or made up by you, that foreshadows the adult actions and gives them more credence? In other words, given the story, what makes these people tick the way they do?

One of the most dramatic examples of this is found in Shakespeare's *Richard III*, a play that purports to be history but is actually more propaganda than anything else. The playwright made his Richard a hunchback with a deformed spine and subsequently fills him with self-loathing. It is a masterful portrait and very much pleased Shakespeare's patron, Queen Elizabeth I, whose grandfather, Henry VII, had mounted a rebellion and taken both Richard's crown and life from him on Bosworth Field. In this case the fiction is absolutely contrary to what historical research tells us, for an exhumation of Richard III's bones showed him to be every bit as straight and tall as any other Plantagenet ruler! But the ploy works on stage to this day, more than four hundred years later, and certainly satisfied the granddaughter of the usurper back when it was written.

Seminal aspects of character development don't have to come from physical circumstances; it's equally valid to use psychological insights where your characters are concerned. For example, one of the givens of the Camelot myth is that King Arthur's wife, Guinevere, falls in love with her husband's best friend and warrior, Lancelot. Over the centuries Guinevere and Lancelot have become synonymous with romantic, but forbidden, love.

At the same time much of the power and poignancy of the story is derived from the fact that everyone roots for Arthur as well. Rather than being portrayed as an ogre his wife would rightfully want to escape, he is generally seen as a respected and admirable character. In most versions both he and Guinevere are adored by their people; very few portray him as wishy-washy, mean or vindictive. And almost none suggests he would consider putting Gwen aside, either for infidelity or her inability to have children.

So the challenge for me was how to make Gwen vulnerable to Lancelot without casting Arthur in a bad light or making her an adulterous floozy. In the end I gave her a childhood love that is not only unfulfilled, it has no closure; the boy runs away, disappearing overnight, and is eventually presumed dead. But I made that character so similar to Lancelot in looks, the first time Gwen sees Lance, she thinks he is Kevin come back to life.

All of this was strictly my own device, but it sets up the attraction without detracting from anyone's moral or ethical standing and adds the human element that euhemerists are always looking for.

Remember, when you're working on a familiar story, don't hesitate to explore or invent background circumstances that throw a new light on the tale—as long as it's a fable.

If it's a verifiable biography you'll need to be more careful about invention; no fair introducing a nasty stepmother if the historical person's real mother actually raised him. Not only are you doing a disservice to your readers by tampering with known history, you also may be inviting a lawsuit.

The original Thomas Wolfe was forever being called into court by outraged friends and neighbors who said his fictional characters were too obviously portraits of themselves. *Kirsch's Handbook of Publishing Law*, by Jonathan Kirsch, lists another, more recent case where the fellow who was the inspiration for a crude and aggressive character in a contemporary *novel* sued the publisher for libel and won, as all he had to prove was that someone else recognized him from the book. The publisher, of course, turned around and sued the author to make her pay the cost! With historical figures you're on firmer ground if they are dead: You can't libel the deceased. But if they aren't well interred, or you bring in their still living descendents, be careful.

When you have no historical record to go on, the author's creative ingenuity should be allowed free reign. If you're dealing with people from the Dark or Middle Ages, chances are you have only the bare bones of the story, and those parts kept alive by biased historians, so you have far more latitude. If you're looking at Lola Montez or Teddy Roosevelt, however, most of their lives and times have been documented. As a result, you have the advantage of a solid reference structure but not much chance to be as free with your imagination as you might like.

Either way, remember to keep your tale within the scope of the believable so you don't strain the thread you're spinning for the reader.

WHEN THE CHARACTERS DRIVE THE PLOT

Sometimes when I'm chatting with friends, something one of them says or does will make me think, *Hey, there's a novel in that.*

Usually the thought is triggered by a circumstance or abstract dynamic, such as a person who becomes so obsessed with his particular demon, he's willing to forfeit not only his own but everyone else's life to the cause—like Captain Ahab in *Moby Dick*. Or I'll get caught on the question of what happens to a free-spirited individual who has to cope with severe social disapproval, such as Hester Prynne in *The Scarlet Letter*.

This novel by Nathaniel Hawthorne is considered one of the finest American historicals ever written, though it is more a psychological study of guilt than what we usually think of as historical fiction. Hawthorne, who was born in 1804, was fascinated by Colonial days and writing since early childhood and had become so familiar with that culture, he could sit down and write his first (and greatest) novel in less than six months—and this before typewriters, even.

It is this total "at homeness" with the era (as well as insights into human nature) that make it such a powerful work. Not only did he capture the attitudes and the lifestyle of the time, he brought the right characters into juxtaposition with exactly the right era so that each heightens the dramatic tension with the other.

DIFFERENT TIMES, DIFFERENT MORES

Most probably you chose your era because it supported either your character or your story best. But sometimes that very choice will impose certain limitations on you. For instance, a bawdy serving wench is likely to be found in Britain during the Elizabethan or Restoration Ages. A girl of that nature born into Cromwell's Commonwealth would probably have been forced to become sly, secretive and cunning rather than forthright and open: She'd giggle rather than laugh full-heartedly and might well be suspect among her peers.

During the Classical Age in Greece, middle- and upper-class women were almost entirely sequestered, had no political or economic voice and were considered nothing more than breeders of the next generation; a man's deepest love was reserved for another man. So it is little wonder that both the stories and history of that time relate almost entirely to men. This worked well for Mary Renault because she had an abiding contempt for women, but for another author it wouldn't work at all.

Getting around these cultural limitations can lead to ingenious solutions on the part of the author. For instance, the protagonist in Nora Lofts's *The Lute Player* is a hunchback woman in Princess Berengaria's medieval court at Navarre. Because of her deformity, the hunchback is seen as neuter, and no one worries that she'll be raped or seduced. Therefore she can come and go with relative impunity, something usually denied women of that place and time.

So believably does Lofts present the world of Richard the Lion-Heart through the eyes of this character, it comes as a surprise to discover the hunchback is purely a literary device. She is a fictional character dropped into the historically real world in order to tell the story with the immediacy of first person by someone with far greater freedom than the actual historical subject would have had.

This technique, by the way, can be very effective if you are writing a plot- or history-driven work. It also allows you to study what actually happened at one step by having the fictional character reacting to what the real people do. In a character-driven story, they would all be fictional characters reacting mostly to each other, but the history itself would not be the main story.

Regardless of whether a work is character or plot driven, fictional characters usually don't interfere with history, though occasionally they may cause something to happen or explain an otherwise murky situation.

In *The Prince and the Pauper*, Mark Twain created a fictionalized adventure for a street urchin who is mistaken for Henry VIII's son Edward and takes his place at court while the real prince shivers in the gutter. Although the boys eventually resume their rightful places, Edward's health is broken and he dies in his early teens. Twain hints that his demise was in part brought on by the experience of living in the real world, which is a far more romantic idea than the view accepted by most historians that the boy-king succumbed to congenital syphilis inherited from his father.

WHERE DO ALL THESE PEOPLE COME FROM?

Clearly all fictional characters begin in the storyteller's mind. Sometimes they evolve slowly, sometimes in the blink of an eye, sometimes against our will as much as because we went seeking them. A few will be patient and plot abiding, while others threaten to run away with the story, the other characters and your heart. (Beware of these last, as they can sidetrack a good book faster than anything else.) But even when I'm fighting with an unruly character, I remember a mother's day card once sent with deepest love and mirth: "A Mother is like an artist . . . she shouldn't have to explain her creations." And as with real children, sometimes the fictional offspring take on lives of their own.

Not infrequently it's memories of our own family and experience that provide inspiration for the characters that go on to become the most interesting. Scarlett O'Hara was said to be derived from Margaret Mitchell's Irish grandmother who survived both the Civil War and Reconstruction to bring her family out on top when so many other, more aristocratic clans were destroyed by the conflict.

How closely Mitchell followed her ancestor's activities is uncertain, but it is known she worried considerably that her first husband would sue her for using him as the prototype of Rhett Butler!

(Authors are notorious for mining their own lives for material, which I don't happen to think is a bad thing. If the artists' purpose in life is to hold a mirror up to reality, how else are we to judge reality but through our own experiences? You do need to be careful not to expose others to ridicule, however. While Thomas Wolfe wrote a great first novel about his family, his portrayal was so unflattering, it's no accident a following book was entitled *You Can't Go Home Again.*)

Other characters develop out of pure concept; you're looking for someone who represents or embodies something specific, such as Ned Tucker in *Sierra.* Born at the end of the Emigrant Trail and orphaned early on, he rides for the Pony Express, takes part in the Civil War and on his way home, herds cattle on the first of the great drives up to Abilene. He's young, energetic, willing to be part of the Union but anxious—after seeing the East—to return to the mountains, which are his natural as well as spiritual home. Curious, ingenious, brave, determined and individualistic, he clearly represents the first generation of Yankee Californians. That's a lot for a single character to carry, but the time line worked out perfectly, and he established himself early on in the book.

Some characters come about after years of study. Mary Renault delved so deeply into the world of Alexander the Great, she was able to people his whole family with living creations. Not only did she write several novels based on his life and loves, her biography, *The Nature of Alexander*, is still considered a definitive nonfiction work on the man himself.

I know one author who gets inspiration from looking at the poster art of Toulouse-Lautrec, and another who scans old phone books looking for interesting or inspiring names. So how you go about developing characters is pretty much your business. Of course, if you've been making up stories much of your life (and most novelists have), you've probably already got a cast of characters stashed away in notebooks, memories and occasional dreams, just waiting for you to call them forth.

LINING UP YOUR CAST

Once you've decided on the era, characters and events, there's still one important question to nail down: Who does the reader root for and why? It's one of the first things agents look for, and if you don't have a quick, firm answer, chances are you have a series of character vignettes rather than a cohesive novel.

Protagonists come in many sizes and shapes, but they all have one thing in common—we care about them. Usually it's because we identify with them; it's no accident that romance heroines are generally portrayed as alone in the world, feel plain, helpless or swamped, and yearn quietly for true love. We've all felt that way at one time or another, after all, which is why romance writers sell tons of books.

In *The Shell Seekers* Rosamunde Pilcher gave us an older woman, ill at ease with the present and her own children, trying to make peace with her life. While Pilcher captured an era that fascinates many younger readers, she also appeals to those who actually lived through World War II, were shaped by an older, deeper morality, and find today's society disturbingly shallow, rootless and selfish.

With *Doctor Zhivago* Pasternak created a caring, sensitive "everyman" who was orphaned at an early age and constantly buffeted by events beyond his control. Who doesn't empathize with that?

And Scarlett O'Hara in *Gone With the Wind* may seem an unlikely choice for a protagonist as she's scheming, manipulative and totally selfish, but the book came out at a time when the country was struggling to survive the Great Depression, and the idea of an indomitable young woman who survives the destruction of her world and rises to meet new challenges inspired a whole generation with hope, if not niceness.

This doesn't mean you should do a market analysis before you start your novel; just keep in mind who the main characters are and why the reader will care about them.

Now's the time to consider the villain as well. Villains also come in a variety of sizes and shapes and are useful in many ways. Generally they represent the conflict aspect of the story, in one way or another.

Sometimes the villain is presented as the personification of evil, a direct conflict character that you can spot (and dislike) immediately. For the Guinevere trilogy I used a historical personage who even now, fifteen hundred years later, still has a bad name among the Welsh. Introduced as Gwen's cousin in the first book, Maelgwn kidnaps and rapes her in the second. In this I remained faithful to the dynamics of the traditional legend, though identifying her kidnapper with that historical person was my own idea.

In order to distance the reader as much as possible from the villain (essentially setting him apart from the rest of humanity in the book) I made no effort to get into Maelgwn's mind, laid no sympathy on his doorstep and made him as despicable as possible without becoming a caricature.

Boris Pasternak used several villains to represent the conflicts of the era in *Doctor Zhivago.* Lara's revolutionary husband grows from an innocent idealist to a frightening creature who symbolizes the breakdown of civilization—the social reformer who loses touch with his own humanity and (perhaps) ends up baying with the wolves in an ice-covered conclusion. Although his presence poses a threat to the lovers, he is far more powerful as an icon of obsessive idealism.

On the equally symbolic but less mythic level is the cynical lawyer who uses Lara and her mother to his own ends and later reappears in time to rescue Lara from the snowbound dasha where she and Zhivago are hiding. The fact that he seems to allow her child to be lost later casts him back into the heartless role, and in the long run one sees him more as a realistic villain than as an archetype. He does, however, further the story.

Some authors let their villains show the other side of the coin. Parke Godwin never has an all-bad villain any more than he has an all-good hero. In his Robin Hood books the more mercurial

Sheriff of Nottingham is in many ways more interesting than the stouthearted, complacent Robin, which works very well. Godwin not only builds a memorable character, he creates a strikingly original read this way.

How human do you want to make your villain? That largely depends on your story, your own taste in reading and what the villain represents. In *Sierra* I have a single wretch who manages to louse up everyone's lives. He is random evil, the bad thing that happens even to nice people, whether they deserve it or not. As a result I've given him very little in the way of background and almost no space as a main, point-of-view character. Everyone else in the book reacts to him, and it shouldn't take the reader long to recognize that whenever this person makes an appearance, bad things are going to happen. In a sense he's the literary equivalent of the shark music from the movie *Jaws*.

If you're a fairly compassionate person, or one obsessed with realism, you can always employ the technique of unmasking the villain at the end of the story, making her actions comprehensible, if not admirable. I used this in the Guinevere trilogy for Morgan le Fey, who ranks second only to Agamemnon's wife, Clytemnestra, as one of the great villainesses of all time. But it seems to me that Morgan's rage against Arthur is fully understandable when she is seen as the abandoned child whose mother ships her away to make room for a new husband and the infant Arthur. Morgan would certainly not be the first adult to turn the pain of rejection into anger: The bible says Cain went through a similar process. That such people cause irreparable harm is part of life; how much you want to make the reader sympathize with them is up to you as an author.

Not all books have specific villains. Melanie Hamilton can hardly be called a villain, though she's nominally the agent of conflict that keeps Scarlett from getting what she wants in *Gone With the Wind*. Certainly the North, the Civil War and the corrupt or greedy carpetbaggers are all villainous forces, but the personification of these are fleeting at best: an anonymous soldier stealing Mama's earrings; the white-trash Jonas Wilkerson trying to steal Tara for taxes; a couple of rogue slaves, recently freed, who attack Scarlett as she drives out to the mill. The convict master who starves and beats his charges is both evil and villainous, but he's employed more to show Scarlett's lack of scruples than as a creature who threatens the protagonist herself.

Thus Mitchell provides us with a series of minor villains who pose a kind of continuing threat to Scarlett and Tara but never assume the proportions of a classic bad guy. This is far more realistic and, given the not-always-savory nature of Scarlett, is perhaps the best way to handle things.

♦ ♦ ♦

So far we've been looking at the evolution of plot, characters and history or cultural background. These are just the bare bones, so to speak, the foundation and essentials necessary before you start writing.

But a novel is a growing thing; people appear, subplots develop and ongoing research brings up a whole new sequence you hadn't expected. It's a rare author who can have everything in place before the start of writing, and an even rarer (and probably much duller) book that comes out exactly as the author originally envisioned it. Consequently, my best advice is, when you have this much of your work organized, it's time to start thinking about how to present your story and what to put on paper.

 Occasionally you'll hear an author say that she just sits down at the keyboard and lets the characters go wherever they will. A few such writers get lucky and have a success or two, but most just end up with unsalable exercises in writing. So if you plan to make a career of this and actually become a "pro," it's important that you develop your ability to plan out and outline your story ahead of time. It may take you months—even years—to get a firm grip on your material, but the tightening and balancing of the overall book is worth it and will result in a much better sale, to say nothing of saving you much time in the actual writing.

THE OUTLINE—A ROAD MAP FOR WHERE YOU'RE GOING

I tend to think of story as what happens to the characters, and plot as the way in which you reveal that to your readers. Thus you, as the author, need to have the story down pat, then use your best storytelling talents to decide who learns what and when—before you begin to write anything. One of the most traditional ways of doing this is to create an outline.

The classic outline has headings numbered *1, 2, 3*, etc., under which are listed the subtexts as A, B, C and so forth. It's a good clean way to get your material down on paper and helps you take stock of what you have.

For me outlining helps create a bridge between story and plot. Thus for *Sierra* I used it in the early phases, when I was developing what happened to the different characters in which years. For instance, the Richards family leaves Springfield, Illinois, early in April 1846 and has to wait over at Independence. My outline for this section looked as follows:

Richards Family—Pioneers

I. Held up at Independence along with hundreds of other emigrants waiting for weather to change. Establish mood of camp, camaraderie of situation, roughness of Independence as compared to Springfield, through Danny's eyes.

II. Danny meets Mort and Zeke Beeker in town.

   A. Whore throwing Mort's boots out of window, Danny amazed at seeing a real, live, "fallen woman."

   B. Zeke brags and lies, but Danny too innocent to see. Danny impressed by boy his own age being so worldly. Mort angry at Indian, hamstrings his horse in revenge.

   C. Danny runs away, afraid townspeople will think he's involved. First confrontation with senseless cruelty—deeply upset by it. Dives headlong into tent, hardly noticing his mother sitting on campstool nearby.

III. Eliza (Danny's mother) is sewing baby clothes with Mary Tucker, the young bride who's pregnant. Comments smugly on challenge of raising boys—doesn't realize Danny's horizons already broadening in the most alarming ways.

(This is a considerably fleshed out version; in actuality it was more just shorthand that noted the important things—Danny's innocence, Zeke's lies, Mort's cruelty, Danny's reaction and his mother's happy obliviousness—rather than whole sentences. But you get the idea.)

Outlines can be extensive and cover the length of the whole book, or they can be, as this one is, simply focusing on a single chapter. Certainly you need some kind of signposts to mark your trail and help you stay on course as you go along. But for me, though I use outlines for planning individual chapters, I find "carding" to be the most useful technique for organizing the overall book.

CARDING YOUR MATERIAL

One big problem with outlines lies in their bulkiness; changing the sequence of your story leads to pages covered with crosshatching, arrows and interpolations so you either have to rewrite it or find a rope to follow the route through the maze. Putting it into a computer that allows several files to be open at once can help, but a quick glance across a paper-strewn worktable is often easier than scrolling up or down on your screen when looking for the next section.

You may find using 3″ × 5″ index cards much easier. Once I know pretty much who does what to whom, I sit down and note each scene in just a word or two on one of these cards, then begin laying them out in different patterns and sequences, much like games of solitaire.

Because there were so many characters and stories woven together in the last of the Guinevere books, it took almost two hundred cards with cryptic messages such as "Mordred arrives" or "Gwen finds out about Elaine" or "The Quest proposed" to get the whole story out on the table where I could organize it.

I also color coded them according to theme: All the scenes relating to Arthur and his son, Mordred, had a bright red felt-tipped pen stripe along the top. Those that dealt with Gwen and Lancelot had a blue stripe, those of the Grail a green one, Morgan le Fey the black one and so on. As a result, once they were laid out it was easy to see what sort of patterns were developing: if there was too big a section between reminders of a coming attraction, when different stories were interfering with each other and whether too many of one color had clumped together before the climactic scene actually arrived.

This visual web of development is a major help for balancing a complex story. And the use of cards allows you to move, delete or put in whole sections with ease and clarity. No more thumbing through ragged pages with scribbles everywhere.

(By the way, it's far easier to find things if you only use one side of a sheet of paper for notes—wasteful, if you're the sort who's ecologically caring, but constantly having to turn pages over to check the information on the reverse side is guaranteed to be time-consuming and confusing.)

When you find a card arrangement that satisfies you, lightly pencil in the numerical sequence in an upper corner so that once you take up the cards, you can lay them back out again in the proper order. Then as you go along telling your story you have only to consult the next card to see which theme to concentrate on next.

Naturally, if something happens during the writing and a character you killed off in the original chapter three comes back with a vengeance in chapter thirty, you can always make further cards for him in order to trace his actions in chapters thirty-one, thirty-two and so forth.

GETTING OUT OF YOUR HEAD AND ONTO THE PAPER

As Dibell points out in her book *Plot*, there's only so much you can do beforehand; writing is as much a question of discovery as it is inspiration. Then, too, authors who keep avoiding putting the words on paper never have a chance to discover what all is inside their stories, their characters and themselves.

So whether you use an outline format, a carding system, a simple list of events or any combination of these three, once you have your map laid out and you've shown enough discipline to start organizing your book, it's time to just plain get on with it.

CHAPTER EIGHT

Bring on the Words

The storyteller's life can be great fun; not only do you get to do something you love, the uninitiated think you make tons of money, the observant see you following your own clock and going your own places and when you get published all sorts of people stop you on the street and tell you how much they like your writing. What no one ever sees is how much work actually goes into putting those words on paper.

There are certain basic problems even longtime professionals run into again and again; they simply come with the territory, and if you're having trouble with some of them, it may be comforting to know you're not alone.

Among the most common problems authors grumble about is that of "getting into the book." The reader who voices the same complaint means he can't get enthusiastic about the characters or story, but the writer means something totally different, and much more difficult to explain. The author may be full of enthusiasm, ideas and energy but still find that no two segments hang together properly. You can produce tens of pages a day, yet still be locked out of your characters' world. Ray Bradbury called it trying to find the hole in the paper.

Exactly what is required to break through that barrier and get into a book I'm not sure, but I suspect that different things work for different writers, and probably the "open sesame" is different with each book as well. What I do know is that even if you have a blazing beginning, a smash prologue or first couple of pages, it's not uncommon to find that what comes next is so much corned beef hash.

Don't feel bad; that's what first drafts are for. Get your opening chapter down on paper, then go back and see what you've got. If it seems like a tangle of spaghetti, welcome to the club. Chances are your difficulties are based on two common situations that are easy to fix, though they take some perseverance.

FINDING THE VOICE

It's hard to pin down exactly what constitutes the voice of a book since it's not something as obvious as content or structure. It may be a particular cadence or rhythm, a subtlety of pace, sometimes even a vocabulary of its own, but it's there, at least in its creator's mind, and it sets that work apart from all others. Finding that voice can be difficult, however, and there's little you can do except keep writing until it begins to *sound* right to you.

Like limbering up stiff muscles or breaking in a pair of old-fashioned shoes, it can sometimes take a lot longer than you expect. If you're having trouble developing your book's voice, keep on writing anyhow, working on new material as much as possible so you don't get stuck forever in one chapter. Even if the voice hasn't taken shape in thirty or forty pages, various other technical matters will have been dealt with, so your time and energy won't have gone for naught.

Margaret Mitchell wrote the last scene of *Gone With The Wind* first, then went back and started her story at the beginning. There may be some advantage in that, both because it gives you something clear to aim toward and a voice to work in. So if you find you're having trouble moving out of the initial pages, go ahead and try to write the end first. If you don't like it, no one has to see it, after all.

You'll know it when you've found the voice. It may come as a sudden epiphany—I looked at a paragraph of short, sharp sentences full of teeth, not lyricism, and knew I'd finally found the voice of *Sierra*—or it may be a gradual growing-into-itself sort of thing. But no matter how or when you recognize it, once you've discovered it you have only to listen to your own ear to be sure you're staying on track through the rest of the work. You can roam back and forth inside the landscape of the work, addressing problems in earlier chapters with confidence and impunity, knowing it will all come out as a whole in the end.

SETTING THE PACE

The other area that can give you grief when you're trying to get into a book has to do with pace. You may have fallen into that classic trap and tried to stuff everything into the first chapter.

You know this is your trouble if you find your sentences are too long and complex, your themes too diverse, the thread you're spinning too full of knots or tangles. If you stand back and look at it, chances are you'll see that the fix is as simple as spreading things out.

Remember that you've got hundreds of pages still before you, and while it's all marching around in your head more or less simultaneously, readers need to discover things one at a time, enjoying the process as they go along.

The term "pace" refers both to the fast/slow rhythms within a novel and the overall effect of the book. The pace of their storytelling varies from author to author; one may become slow and thoughtful in the midsections of her work, while another skims over the surface of everything, dashing from point to point so quickly the reader has no sense of depth or content. Some of it is the individual artist's way of expressing himself; some is the result of too much editing out or adding to; and many of the worst cases could have been avoided by outlining the work at the start.

Whether you're going back over the first draft and recognizing that you need to add balance to what you've already done or you're trying to plan where you're going next, take the time to assess just what is happening to the arc of your book.

The arc is the dynamic forward motion that carries readers from one major crisis and completion to another. In many ways it's similar to the arc of a musical composition, and it involves seeing where the dramatic moments come, how to build on them, when to give the reader a rest, what the climax or high point of your story is and how it ends. Charting the various conflicts may help you see the arc of the story as well as how to get the most out of your plot and characters, for you want to keep the reader interested and satisfied with the drama.

Keep in mind that this is the biggest difference between fiction and nonfiction, storytelling and reporting: The journalist reports what is going on, whereas the novelist has the characters act out the story. This allows the reader to experience the story with the characters; it's what gets people hooked and gives them a sense of catharsis by the end. So when you're outlining your arc, go for the dramatic moments and keep your characters fully involved. Check out *Writing the Blockbuster Novel*, by Al Zuckerman, for more on drama, arc and pace.

One of the most unusual aspects of Zuckerman's book is his inclusion of four different outlines of Ken Follett's novel, *The Man from St. Petersburg.* It took Follett a year—and a total of ten outlines—to develop and perfect the final story, and you can see how he changed, tightened, expanded and refocused both the characters and plot in the various revisions. If you read the actual novel as well, you'll find he improved it even more during the writing. As Zuckerman suggests, studying the evolution of this work is an education in itself, and well worth the time involved.

WHOSE STORY IS THIS, ANYWAY?

Before you even begin writing, you'll need to decide who's telling your story, whose shoulder are you looking over, whose head are you in. This is known as the "point of view" (POV) and needs to be established early on, both for your sake and the readers'.

Omniscient POV

Omniscient author is the most common POV, and often the most fun to work with as you can be anywhere at any time, tell about a diversity of people all doing things simultaneously, even sample their inner thoughts and feelings. Certainly the omniscient author is one of the most popular and frequently used POVs, probably because it is about as close as one can come to playing God.

As with every decision in writing, it has its advantages and drawbacks. The reader gets to know that catastrophe is approaching even as the hero goes blithely about his business; the story can be advanced on several fronts at once, and you can develop a complexity of tastes, rather like the range of flavors found in a good stew. On the other hand, it lacks the intimacy possible with first person and becomes an easy vehicle for digressions simply because you can be everywhere (and everyone) at once.

If you're of a philosophical bent, any comments you make are likely to be seen as "author intrusion," a decided no-no that theoretically breaks the magic of your thread and snaps the reader out of the world you've set up. When *The French Lieutenant's Woman* came out to rave reviews, most everyone noted that the author, John Fowles, had suddenly intruded himself about three-quarters of the way through, clearly a breach of contract with the reader. But it worked so well, everyone also made an exception for it. I personally have never seen anything wrong with author comments and asides, as long as they are of a philosophic nature, not long lectures; after all, Hawthorne did it. But some agents and editors are put off if you slip even little ones in, so be forewarned.

Somerset Maugham, who wrote *The Moon and Six Pence* (the novel biography about Gauguin), *Of Human Bondage* and *The Razor's Edge* was a master storyteller from the first half of the twentieth century who frequently got around this by using a first-person narrator telling the story of the characters. That allows the author to make all sorts of comments as the outside observer/philosopher and still tell the story in the third person. This technique may seem dated and slow paced next to the frantic action and reaction we're more accustomed to at the end of this century, but Maugham's ability to capture human nature in a net of words is timeless.

First-Person POV

Another way to get around the problem of "author intrusion" is by using first-person point of view since the person you're speaking for can make all sorts of comments and asides as part of her persona. As with anything else, there are both pros and cons with this choice, but I find it far more fluid than most and used it for all three of my Guinevere books.

For one thing, it allows you to build your character from the inside out, sharing numerous observations that would not be acceptable from the omniscient author. I also made my Gwen a homely tomboy from the North so that she would be an outsider to Arthur's world and therefore able to see, inquire about and respond to everything more vividly than she would have if she'd been raised inside the system.

That word, *inside*, has a lot to do with reader response. First person is far more intimate and immediate than other POVs; the reader is instantly in the head and world of the narrator. For instance, Mary Renault's *The Bull From the Sea* begins

> It was dolphin weather, when I sailed into Piraeus with my comrades of the Cretan bull ring. Knossos had fallen, which time out of mind had ruled the seas. The smoke of the burning Labyrinth still clung to our clothes and hair.

This is the second of two books told by Theseus, slayer of the minotaur and soon to be ruler of Athens. In this deceptively simple first paragraph the author sets the scene, locale and connection with the great palace of Knossos on Crete, which was destroyed at the end of the first book. For those who have read *The King Must Die*, it follows right on. For those who are coming to Renault's work new, just enough has been said to pique the interest, but not enough to bog the reader down; the story, after all, still lies ahead, for Theseus is still a young man.   •

The same information conveyed from the third-person distance of the omniscient author wouldn't be nearly as effective.

First-person POV does have a major drawback, however. Whereas the omnipotent author can be any- and everywhere, first person limits you to one location (wherever your character is at the moment), and you can't clue in the reader about what else is going on until or unless your character knows about it as well.

I ran into this problem in the first of my Guinevere books, *Child of the Northern Spring*. I wanted the audience to understand Arthur's rise to power as well as Gwen's background so the readers would know where each was coming from when the two met.

That's easier said than done when you're limited to first person, and my very patient editor sent back three chapters that were basically long reports by Arthur's childhood friend about the young king's earlier adventures. It seems you can't do that, either, so I had to find other ways to convey the information to both Gwen and the reader.

The upshot for first-person POV is you either take your character to the action, bring the action to him or have him react to the results; you can't have someone else spend fifteen or twenty pages explaining what happened elsewhere. I've never quite understood why that's not allowed, but you can save yourself some real grief by avoiding it from the beginning.

Multiple POVs

Yet another way to tell your tale is with multiple points of view. Using this approach, you basically get inside different characters at different times in the book. There are both dangers and delights to this. Some agents are death on the subject while others don't seem to mind, and Al Zuckerman encourages it in his book, *Writing the Blockbuster Novel*.

A close examination of *Gone With the Wind* shows that Margaret Mitchell, who stayed over the shoulder of Scarlett most of the time, did occasionally slide into other POVs, usually getting into the heads of male characters. For instance, when Scarlett is setting out to sell herself to Rhett for the tax money, Mitchell goes into Ashley's thoughts; he knows full well what Scarlett is going to do, and while castigating himself for not being able or willing to stop her, he admires her "bravery and courage." The section lasts less than a page and gives one a new insight into that famous southern gentleman—on the one hand he's far more attuned to what Scarlett really is than one might have expected, and on the other, quite capable of deluding himself that she's being noble and self-less when she sets out to seduce Rhett.

The second sequence is when Frank Kennedy, the fiancé Scarlett stole from her sister, decries the fact that he can't control his new wife. One feels his frustration at not being able to keep her at home, away from the lumber mills, and following ladylike pursuits. He's worried about what other men will say, as well as the danger she invites, but is even more afraid of angering her by putting his foot down.

Both sections give the reader a new perspective on Scarlett and the weaknesses or confusions of her men that couldn't have been seen if everything was noted from Scarlett's POV.

Some authors use several POVs to flesh out major characters. In both *Sherwood* and *Robin and the King*, Parke Godwin occasionally shifts POV to different minor characters in order to give a description, background or broader perspective to the reader. Again, these are short passages, such as interior musings, journal entries or letters, that are dropped into the middle of much longer chapters, and they go a long way toward adding texture, information and pace.

An entire episode that would have taken up two or three chapters in acting out can be given to the reader in a short letter, for instance, that furthers the plot and pace at the same time introducing a fresh voice. (More of this in the next chapter on keeping up the pace.) But even as multiple POVs add variety of tone and perspective, they need to keep the focus on either a major character or the plot so as not to become digressions.

Sometimes an author will use several different points of view within the same novel as a whole style, not just a bit of color. This can be very interesting, provided the writer makes each character separate and distinct.

Virginia Woolf's *The Waves*, while being more a literary tour de force than a proper historical, is a remarkable example of this, and anyone interested in a wordsmith's exuberant plying of her craft should take the time to explore it. In this work each section starts with a brief stream-of-consciousness sequence by an unnamed character. There are five major characters who grow up together, and the crux of the book is how they each react to a sixth character—an outsider who plays a crucial role in the lives of each of them. The reader never gets inside this outsider's head, never knows the who or what or why of his character, but vividly feels the reactions of the quintet to his presence or absence. Although Woolf never specifies which character a chapter is beginning with, you soon develop such a familiarity with the individual stream-of-consciousness voices, you always know who is doing the thinking.

To me there's nothing wrong with multiple POVs, provided it's clear to the reader whose head you're in at any one time. Occasionally authors will use two different POVs in alternate chapters. That's fine, but you need to remember to communicate who is telling which part of the tale, particularly if all the chapters are in first person. Usually a simple name under the chapter number or title will suffice to alert the reader.

 So far we've been talking about voice, pace and POVs, all of which are things that will come up as soon as you sit down to write. Still, getting your people from your mind to the page is ususally not difficult; doing it in a way that results in a novel can be something else again. If you've already made several forays into your work and discovered that the resultant vignettes or scenes are alright on their own, but just don't hang together as a book, take heart.

Most of that can be corrected with organization, discipline and keeping a firm eye on where you want to go. One of the easiest ways to do that is to break down the project into more manageable units. So here are a few tips for creating order out of chaos. They are certainly worth a try.

CHAPTER BY CHAPTER

Although I find traditional outlines too rigid for the overall organization of my novels, I certainly use them on a segment by segment basis. Or you can use the carding technique. The most important thing is that you decide what the point of the scene or segment is, who can best tell or show it and what kind of ending, resolution or hook is involved at the end.

Blocking Out Scenes

This is a theatrical technique that can be useful for those who want to keep a tight rein on their material. In this system you sit down and list exactly who does what, introduces which and goes where— all in the most dramatic sequence—before you even start to put words to the situation. It's a help for polishing highly dramatic scenes and makes sure you get the most out of each entrance, exit and aside.

I personally find that too confining, as though everything is so carefully mapped out, there's no creative zest to what I put on the paper. So I work on a pattern of knowing where my characters are at the beginning and where they need to be at the end of a chapter, or even a scene, but how they get there is pretty much up to them. That's where I get the creative kick, as they often come up with some wonderful surprises. At the same time, as long as they get where I expected them to be at the end, we're still telling the same story.

Choosing Chapter Titles

Chapter titles are an excellent way to keep you focused when it comes to actually writing. Although most novels don't use chapter titles and I hadn't planned on them, when the editor of the first Guinevere book asked me to put them in, it proved to be a difficult task. Most of the chapters wandered all about, and though they always furthered the story, it was hard to say what the specific subjects of some of them were. So when it came to the second volume, I deliberately picked a chapter name (character, place or event) BEFORE writing that segment. It's a tip worth passing on because it focuses your attention, the main point of the chapter is always in mind and the end result will be that much more professional. Even if the title never sees the light of print, it will make your writing both smoother and easier.

DRAFT BY DRAFT

Different writers commit their stories to paper in different ways. Several authors I know write out the first draft by hand. One uses a yellow legal pad for the day's original work, then edits it with lines, arrows, crosshatches and what have you and types that up on green paper—draft two, easy to spot. When he has a sufficient stack of green pages, he edits them and retypes the finished product on white paper.

Authors of this stripe tend to be careful about every word choice, often do only a few pages a day and sweat blood in the process because they don't want to keep retyping the same pages over and over. Those of us who write at computer keyboards tend to be profligate by comparison, with many rewrites simply because it's so easy to push a button and have a machine type out a whole page. The big problem for us is how to keep all those different drafts separate but available. The information below about chapter headings works just as well for the typist as it does for the computer whiz, but it is geared specifically for the management of your manuscript inside that magic box. While it doesn't get into the fine points of using a computer, it does come from years of trial and error in keeping track of various drafts.

Make a New File for Each Chapter

While chapter breaks are a matter of taste for each author, most books have a number of them, and it's a lot easier to save or search individual chapters of seven to thirty pages than it is to deal with the entire manuscript of three or four hundred pages. Besides, if you wipe out a file, you haven't lost the whole thing.

Name Your Files

The key to retrieving your files is in the naming of them, because unless you have some basic system, you'll find yourself staring blankly at a directory that might as well be a Chinese laundry list. I use letters to designate the version of the book, and numbers for each chapter, followed by the date. Thus the first draft of chapter one of this book was "A1. 1/2/96." This file name also becomes the chapter heading in the top right corner of each page so I can be sure I've got the right one in the future.

For anything more than simple changes, copy the first file, re-naming or redating it, and make your corrections in this new file, so the earlier version stays intact. (Don't forget to change the heading on the page, too.)

Believe me, there's nothing more frustrating than having an

editor say, "How about elaborating on that theme in this place?" when you've already done that in an earlier draft but erased, written over or thrown out the result! So save those files; they may come in handy in the future.

If it's a major rewrite or change of plot, I save the new material—with a different letter in the file name . . . i.e. B1. 1/10/96. When I'm satisfied with a whole run of chapters, I make sure they all have the same letter designation. By the time I reach the end of a novel, I'm generally working on version L, M or N. Remember, the letter refers to the most recent draft of the book, not the number of rewrites.

By copying and renaming the past chapters with the present version's letter, they'll all be the same. You won't have to remember that you want the B version of chapters one to six, the F version of seven to twelve and the J version of all the rest. And by putting the alphabetic designation in front of the chapter number it will be easier to sort and collect all the files that begin with the same letter into one folder.

This sounds more cumbersome in explanation than it is in actual practice, and you may devise a different system that works better for you. Just remember that a novel is a "work in progress" until the last page is set in type, so you're bound to have changes, second thoughts and corrections both big and small. This is one way for you to keep it all straight, locate any past file and tell at a glance if you're working on the most current version.

Back Up Your Files

Backups are another basic but important step that will keep your world more secure. Most computers use floppy diskettes, and you'd be wise to make backup disks and stow them somewhere safe. Refrigerators are one of the best places, since they rarely melt in a fire; just make sure to wrap your floppies in plastic so they don't get damp. Also, electronic rights are a big part of current publishing contracts, so some publishers want to have a disk as well as hard copy of your manuscript, and it's easiest if you make them as you go along.

Protect Your Manuscript

Three ring binders—large ones—are indispensable as far as I'm concerned! Once I've printed out a new chapter or section, I store it in the binder along with the other acceptable chapters. If it's a rewrite or renamed version I take the old one out, keeping it safely in a box to one side, and put in the new one. That way if I ever have to run for my life from a tidal wave, I can grab up one binder and know it's got the whole of the manuscript complete and up-to-date.

We never expect calamity to strike; earthquakes, fires and floods happen in books, not to real people, usually. Except sometimes they do. Author and attorney Steve Martini was just completing his second mystery novel when his house burned down. It was clear to the rest of the writing community that he had become more author than lawyer when the most important thing he saved was the manuscript.

GETTING ON WITH IT

Occasionally someone will ask if he has to have a college degree to get published. Believe me, if a publisher has an exciting manuscript in hand, the last thing he cares about is if the author even finished kindergarten. And outside of the experience of campus life and the breadth of cultural information available, college doesn't make any real difference. If you want to read the classic works of literature, you'll get them from the library. And if you want to write novels, you'll pick up books such as this one.

So now that I've done away with the last of your excuses, it's time to get on with the writing. There's still all sorts of stuff to discuss, such as fleshing out your world, foreshadowing events and pacing your work. But these are things most of us learned as we went along . . . and if you can type with one hand and read with the other, you'll have it made.

CHAPTER NINE

The Days of Creation

I t's always interesting to compare working habits, techniques and philosophies with other novelists. Mostly their concerns are to tell a good story well, with believable characters and actions. And for those who write historical fiction, there's the added dimension of creating a world that is different from our own.

Beyond that, there's the challenge of learning more about your characters as you go along, which many authors will tell you is part of the excitement of creativity.

Technical challenges and opportunities come up constantly—how to explore a developing subplot, present this or that idea, get the most out of historical events, find new possibilities or tie something together you hadn't seen before. The result is that no matter how well you plan, you're bound to encounter all sorts of delights and dilemmas you didn't expect. The best I can do is alert you to the most common ones so you'll recognize them when they arise.

ESTABLISHING YOUR WORLD

Good writers achieve a balance somewhere between hand-feeding the readers and believing that it's up to the audience to ferret out the meaning and content of the work. While this last approach was a popular philosophic attitude at one time—make them work to understand and enjoy it—the continual diet of pabulum served up by television has changed that approach.

Television has also created a visually oriented society, used to *seeing* things happen in the comfort of their own living rooms. The result is that those who still read are always, at least subconsciously, looking for a physical description of person and place so they can *see* it in their minds' eyes. Reading a book is such an internal process, it helps to give your audience a means of visualizing your characters and locations.

The description needn't take up much room but should be brought in soon after a person or place is introduced. The very first sentence of *Gone With the Wind* sets up Scarlett's physical presence, saying that she's not really pretty, but none of the men who found her so fascinating noticed that. Mitchell then goes on to describe both Scarlett's shape and coloring, and the clear green eyes that are referred to frequently throughout the work, sometimes directly and sometimes obliquely, as in noting that a new dress set off her eyes wonderfully well.

The same goes for setting the scene. It's important to give the reader a place to stand right from the start, though you don't need to describe it in detail. In the first Guinevere book there is a crucial scene in a room that hadn't been mentioned before. Not wanting to slow the pace by a description, I established that the meeting would be in the State Chamber and later wove a description in the middle of Gwen's reaction when her father tells her she's just been chosen to be King Arthur's wife:

> "What?" The word ricocheted off table and wine flagon, map chest and tile floor.
> "That's what Merlin was here to ask about. . . ."

There you have it. The conversation goes on hot and furious for another couple of pages since Gwen is decidedly not thrilled with the idea, but the reader has some notion of the setting and can furnish the rest to his own liking.

There is, however, the question of how much you bring nature and the countryside to the fore, since characters of an older era would have been at the mercy of both. Setting the scene with landscape descriptions was very much in style in the past, but this century does better with bits of information seen or reacted to by the characters. Thus rather than my describing the environment, it is the stage driver in *Sierra* who notes the hot, dusty smell of late August tarweed and skunk cabbage, or Yury Zhivago in *Doctor Zhivago* who is enthralled by the crystal beauty of ice and snow that shrouds the rooms of the dasha where he and Lara find sanctuary at the end of their relationship. This keeps the reader experiencing the world through the characters, though how much time is spent reflecting on it is entirely up to the author.

Partially this is a question of pace. Paragraphs of expository writing, whether they be of landscape description or historical reporting, slow the story considerably, so you don't want to go overboard. On the other hand, it helps add dimension and emotional identification between the reader and the character because they have now both experienced the same thing.

PORTRAIT OF THE TIMES

Often, if you're writing about a society that is very different from that of your audience, you have to educate your readers without digressing into a sociology lesson. Sometimes that's hard to do.

Remember that people want to read about people, not facts. The moment the author's voice begins to lecture about something, you've broken the spell, forfeited the contract and let go of the thread.

Even two paragraphs of that kind of exposition can bring the story to a screeching halt. The best way to avoid this and still get the information across is through the characters themselves. It can be in dialogue between two people: "How come so-and-so has done such and such?" Or it can be presented in action: "When I heard that such and such took place, I raced back to the farm, afraid that blah-blah-blah. . . ." This last is certainly effective, as long as the explanation of "blah-blah" isn't too long.

Or it can be an interior monologue, such as Columbus mulling over the fact that everyone KNOWS the world is flat, but the ships keep sinking out of sight as they get farther away. This kind of inner musing gives you an opportunity to show just how quick, superstitious, fearful, adventurous or confused your character is, at the same time defining what the rest of his culture accepts or expects—fertile ground for conflict, if you want to pursue it!

John Jakes uses all these teaching techniques in *The Kent Chronicles*, where he deftly weaves fictional and historical characters together in a story that deals with the human reactions to, as well as the historical importance of, certain events. Thus one experiences the horror of what we now call the Battle of Bunker Hill in terms of heat, smoke, sweat, fear and nausea, just as the participants must have. Yet the focus of the reader's interest is slightly off center of the historical event: Yes, Philip Kent feels that he has to serve the cause of liberty, but the reader is equally concerned that Kent survive the British attacks and the flight through the narrows of the Charlestown Neck so he can return to his new wife, who is expecting their first child.

It is this ability to craft a story that brushes up against history but doesn't focus totally on it that makes the series so popular. We learn, in human terms, what is too often presented only as names and dates in history classes.

Jakes also portrays famous people as more or less normal folks, without the aura of importance that history accords them. So when one or another meets the historical moment, it is simply part of the story, not an apex to which the author has been leading us. That apex has to do with the lives of the fictional characters, not the historical turning point, per se. In other words, Jakes always keeps his actors downstage, in front of the scenery.

Remember to give your characters mannerisms or habits consistent with their times. The use of snuff or smelling salts, the adjustment of a toga, the snapping open of a fan—each of these immediately brings to life an era or location and keeps your reader firmly in that make-believe world.

This is the kind of cultural detail to watch for as you do your research; any book dealing with everyday life in your era should have invaluable material for day-by-day detail.

You can also get good ideas from historical vignettes, contemporary art or modern reenactments. Wherever the ideas come from, put them to use. I read in a brochure that Somerset, England, is famous for its cider, and a note on medieval days showed it was strained through goat hair screens. That was so clearly an evocation of preindustrial life, I had my Guinevere checking those filters for breaks or moth holes during a conversation with one of her ladies.

Not only do such details keep your world vividly alive for the reader, if you choose them properly they can say all sorts of things about your characters as well. In this case it shows Gwen as a working queen, setting up the court kitchen for cider making; the concept of a queen being little more than a pretty figurehead is a much later invention.

In *Gone With the Wind* the collecting of jewelry from the Confederate ladies at the ball in Atlanta early in the Civil War is another example of a vignette that shows several personalities and circumstances at once, including Rhett's gallantry toward Melanie when he returns her wedding ring.

Even minor characters can be brought to life by the use of little but timely habits, actions or activities. If you have a fussy Regency dandy who is afraid of germs, give him a large supply of lace-bordered hankies so that he can dust or wipe off all surfaces or hold one to his nose as he hurries away from perceived pestilence. Or if your Roaring Twenties flapper is a vain little minx, let her constantly check her image in the compact she carries in her mesh bag.

Attention to this sort of thing also helps develop loyal fans. When I get fan letters or calls, the readers invariably mention that I created a whole world for them; whether this is rare among modern authors or simply the best thing my readers can think of to say, I'm not sure. But I hear it often enough to conclude it's something that makes a specific impression.

SUBPLOTS AND DIVERSIONS

There's no better place to see how effectively subplots can be used than in *Gone With the Wind*, for just as Mitchell provides an assortment of conflict characters and dozens of devices to establish her time and setting, she also uses subplots with real finesse.

Subplots provide texture, character development, temporary conflicts and, occasionally, necessary education about the culture. Sometimes they become running themes that help give the story continuity.

Early on in the book Scarlett's mother, Miss Ellen, is off on an errand of mercy, delivering the out-of-wedlock baby of Emmie Slattery, a white-trash girl who lives nearby. Miss Ellen is quick to scold Jonas Wilkerson, the father of the baby, for not having married Emmie, and one sees not only Miss Ellen's philanthropy and strong moral stance, but a sniveling portrait of nongentry in antebellum Georgia.

When Scarlett escapes from Atlanta during the burning thereof, she returns to Tara, thankfully finding it still standing. But her mother has just died, having caught typhoid as a result of nursing Emmie and her family through their bout with the illness. Thus the pestilence of white trash moves closer to Scarlett and has become more than a nuisance, having taken Miss Ellen's life.

Later it is Jonas Wilkerson bragging that he is going to buy Tara for the price of the tax bill that galvanizes Scarlett past whatever principles she might still have and sends her off in search of Rhett

Butler. The only reason she doesn't end up in Rhett's bed at that point is the fact that he is himself both broke and incarcerated. She does, however, tell her sister's fiancé a pack of lies in order to marry him herself, thereby using his money to save Tara—and ruining her sister's future.

Thus Mitchell has woven Jonas and Emmie into a running subplot, with the threat they pose to Scarlett (and her reaction to it) becoming stronger with each encounter. They could have been different characters in each sequence, but by making all three threats involve the one white-trash couple, the author made the story tighter and brings home an irony that would have been missed otherwise.

Some subplots can be laid out in the outline stage, while others simply come up during the writing. For instance, while working on *Sierra*, I knew that one of the women would run away from her older and very wealthy husband. B.J. is an earnest fellow who's spent much of his life bailing out the charming, but irresponsible, younger brother their dying father left in his charge. For more than a year I saw the brother Jamie merely as a colorful counterpoint, a way to show both how stiff and rigid B.J. was and partially explain why he was like that.

It wasn't until I started to write out the wife's defection that it dawned on me the younger brother, who until then had never actually appeared on the page, was the perfect one to sweep her off her feet. It was so right, both psychologically and dramatically, I let out a whoop of glee you could hear two counties away. And now the brother's earlier presence in B.J.'s thoughts is more than character contrast; it's foreshadowing as well.

For me this is the kind of unplanned creation that makes writing such a joy and keeps me working at it. Yet whether you stumble on these things accidently or lay them out carefully in advance, this kind of subplot can enrich your book immensely, tightening a sprawling story, adding substance to specific characters and furthering the plot without slowing the pace. Just remember to keep an eye on them.

This last point is important because sometimes subplots turn into digressions, auxiliary stories that get out of hand, digress from your original intent and distract from the main characters.

It's easy to fall prey to such diversions. They can come about because of an unforeseen character, a sudden twist in plot or a new discovery in research, any one of which can be either a major inspiration or a recipe for disaster.

Excited by the prospect, charmed by the new dimension in your story, before you know it you've written forty to sixty pages of totally diversionary stuff. Without realizing it you've led the reader onto a different thread, and instead of weaving in a new strand to strengthen the original story line, you've sidetracked both yourself and your audience to a dead end.

This is another good reason to stick fairly closely to your original outline and arc. If it's a character you've fallen in love with, put her to one side and plan on doing a separate book, at another time, with her in the foreground.

Most digressions are hard to see at the time they captivate you, but if you don't spot them before you get to the completed manuscript, let's hope you have a sharp-eyed agent who will. If you start getting rejection letters saying that you don't have a good enough handle on the story, you can figure it's because you've gone wandering down diversionary trails.

LOVE THOSE LITTLE DARLINGS

Another aspect of writing novels, historical or otherwise, is the question of how you feel about the different characters. Author Jackie Collins once said that she ends up loving all her characters, that she has to, because she gets inside them all. And one of this century's greatest actors, Sir Laurence Olivier, talked about needing to love even the villains you play so you can portray their humanity as well as their evil.

On the one hand, if you live with your characters for months or years at a time, you certainly get to know them inside and out. I often dream about mine when a book is in full swing, and by the time I was finishing up the third Guinevere book, it felt as though I knew those people as well as I knew my own family—maybe better.

With those books there was no trouble loving the people involved, but that's not always the case. Although for the most part the people of *Sierra* have become a pleasure to work with, I had a good deal of trouble with the nominal heroine because she starts out as a spoiled brat. My distaste for her was so strong, my agent picked it up and pointed out that if the author didn't like her, who would? (Since then the book's been restructured, and I don't have as much trouble with her as in the earlier versions.) It is, however, a lesson worth thinking about. Find what is most human, vulnerable or poignant in your characters, or drop them from the story.

Sometimes a character gets out of hand, taking over too much time or space. This is usually how a digression begins, and you need to decide whether you've encountered a stroke of genius or an unruly child. (Ansen Dibell talks about this problem in her book *Plot*, noting that Melville was focusing on a totally different character until several chapters into *Moby Dick*, when he discovered Captain Ahab. Back in those days authors didn't have the luxury of computers and printouts, so the original character continues to take up space early on; nowadays a good editor would have you write him out and bring Ahab to the fore more quickly. Anyhow, that's a case where the digression was, indeed, a stroke of genius, and American literature is the richer for it, by far.)

If you get in this bind, my best advice is to stop and look at your original synopsis every so often. How much have you deviated from it, and have the changes been for the better? You should be able to follow the good strong through line of your story; if you change subjects in midstream, chances are it will be lots weaker and more confusing than your original idea. Either go back and redo the earlier chapters to conform with your new vision, or jettison the diversion and haul that character back into line. It's important to keep an open mind to both possibilities.

THOSE SNEAKY ANACHRONISMS

As mentioned before, anachronisms are the bane of every good historical novelist. They can creep in during the planning stage, the research phase or even as you're writing, and trying to avoid them may cause you to lose the momentum of your story. Sometimes they come not from shoddy research, but from decisions you made earlier in the project, long before you even thought about anachronisms.

For instance, do you attempt to use the language of the time? If you're writing about Elizabethan England, do you use Shakespeare as your guide? And if so, how do you keep it from sounding corny and fake? Do you employ *forsooth* and *oft, verily* and *doth?* And how careful do you have to be about not slipping in twentieth-century words?

To this last I'd say be *very* careful. Convinced that people in every age talk to each other in informal terms, I intentionally used a natural style of conversation in the Guinevere books. Fortunately my editor pointed out that I'd gotten so casual, the modern word *okay* had slipped in several places, introducing a jarring note. So I used my computer to delete the four or five "Okay" responses the word-finder came up with.

But, you guessed it . . . among my first fan letters was one from a librarian in Massachusetts who noted that she had loved the book, until she came to a certain page where Arthur asks Gwen, "Are you okay?" after she's been knocked down by a large dog. Naturally the computer hadn't found it because it was inside a sentence and not capitalized at the beginning. The reader was so upset by this anachronism, she felt compelled to write and tell me. So be very careful about how casual you get, and try to avoid that sort of blunder as you go along.

Which brings up the question of whether to incorporate another country's language; if you have a character who speaks Danish rather than English, how do you indicate that for the reader?

First, it depends on how important it is to the story. Is an inability to communicate crucial to the plot development? If so, go ahead and incorporate whole sentences (without translation); it's bound to frustrate the reader as much as it does the other characters in your book. If it isn't part of the story line, don't do it. It stops the flow of information to the reader, breaks the thread you work so hard to keep strong and may come across as a kind of smug one-upsmanship on the part of the author.

The same holds true of introducing foreign quotes; bits of Latin or other niceties may make the readers feel that you're bragging about your own "inside" knowledge at the same time you're delib-erately serving them something they can't assimilate. Again, if it's important to the story, let the reader in on it; for instance, "He stared at the family crest with its motto of *Never Give In* inscribed in Latin" gets the idea across without raising the readers' hackles.

Parke Godwin used a sprinkling of French or Saxon terms in his Robin Hood books, but only a word or two at a time, and almost always where their meanings could be deduced. Since the conflict of the two cultures was at the heart of his story, it seemed appro-priate to remind the reader occasionally of their difficulty in communicating.

Colleen McCullough's Roman books contain a smattering of Latin phrases, but most all of them are fully defined and fleshed out in her glossary or are self-explanatory in their written context.

In the long run I think it's better to signify different cultures by the occasional use of a familiar phrase in the other language, such as "Madre Mia," "Auf Wiedersehen" or "Voila!"

Every language has its own lilt, rhythm and cadence. If you have a good ear for that sort of thing, give your characters the appropriate melody, in English but with the other language pattern. Used in moderation this can be very effective, though whole sections of out-and-out dialect can spoil an otherwise good read.

Another basic problem that pops up from time to time is that of ascribing today's values to yesterday's culture. At one point someone sent Mary Renault a script about classical Greece that earned a very tart reply because the scriptwriter had assumed that humility was considered a virtue by the Hellenes. In fact it was heroic deeds and acts, along with pride in and responsibility for those actions, that were most admired by that culture, and anyone who was humble was looked upon as spineless and weak. In her reply Renault minced no words in pointing out that it was morally reprehensible as well as unprofessional for the scriptwriter to impose later Christian virtues on the thoroughly pagan Greeks.

So be careful to stay within the mind-set of your era (as Hawthorne did in *The Scarlet Letter*), and do educate your reader as to the same, if it is different from the world we know.

WHOSE REALITY ARE YOU DEALING WITH?

Another conflict one bumps into occasionally is that of historical accuracy vs. the reader's perception. Even though it's a fairly common occurrence, it's safe to say each case needs to be decided on its own merits.

For example, the Cheviot Hills that form the present day border between England and Scotland are famous for being swept by the wind off the North Sea. Devoid of trees, they are covered with a vast carpet of tall grass that ripples and moves in this wind, adding to the strange, magical quality of light and airiness above them. Anyone who has been there is likely to remember that and find any other description to be anachronistic.

But they have only been treeless for the last thousand years. Back in A.D. 500, when my Gwen would have ridden over them, they would have been as heavily wooded as the rest of Britain. (It used to be said that a squirrel could go from the top of England to the bottom without ever touching ground, so thick were the old forests before the coming of the shipbuilding Tudors and the rise in population.)

The question of how to present the Cheviots is an excellent example of the author having to decide between what the contemporary reader experiences and what is historically correct. In the end the contemporary storyteller in me won out, going with what the modern reader knew, though I noted the problem in the preface for those purists who might otherwise feel they needed to point out my error.

There will be a similar though bigger problem in my projected book on the Trojan War, as an early archaeologist erroneously named some antique graves and treasure after the Greek heroes of that conflict. Now it turns out that the well-known Mask of Agamemnon predates the Trojan War by several centuries, as does the Tomb of Clytemnestra. In this case, because more travelers to Greece are likely to know those artifacts than they are to know the actual history, I'll probably fudge a little and use those as the tombs of the battling king and queen.

This is the kind of decision that only the author can make. Ninety-nine percent of the time I am absolutely bound by the reality of what my research turns up. But I am first and foremost a storyteller, not an academic scholar, and the cathartic value of getting good closure on a powerful story is more important to me than being totally faithful to what we know scientifically.

If you have the same feelings, go with what works dramatically and emotionally for you, and explain any anachronisms in the Preface.

Names of cities and rivers are another place you need to make a decision. Mary Stewart said in her Merlin trilogy that she preferred to use the old Roman names for various cities because the modern ones brought up too many images of smokestacks and ugly slums. There certainly is something to that, but I chose to use the modern-day names because my readership is mainly in the States, and if they were to look at a current atlas, or had been to England themselves, this was a way for them to more easily locate where my characters were.

No matter how conscientious the author/researcher or how

much a purist, there are always going to be some things that slip past you. A part of me says, "Enough, already. Do the best you can and let it be." And then I remember reading a fine book that included an extremely powerful re-creation of the crucifixion of Jesus. Clearly, the author had been to Jerusalem, had become thoroughly familiar with her landscape and certainly had captured the feel of it for her reader. But suddenly I was going back and rereading a sentence; did she actually say there were eucalyptus trees in Christ's world?

Unfortunately she did. No doubt she had seen them during her visits to Jerusalem; they are perfect for that kind of climate. But eucalyptus trees are native to Australia and didn't reach any other part of the globe until many centuries later. Nit-picking? Maybe. But as with the *okay* in my book, the presence of those trees on her page jolted me right out of her fictional world and back to present-day reality.

Naturally you can't weed out everything; I'm still discovering anachronisms in my Guineveres some ten years later. But it does pay to screen things as closely as possible. And yes, there are books on what is native flora and fauna and what is introduced when for practically every area in the world.

GIVING YOUR MANUSCRIPT TEXTURE

Lots of times we get so focused on the words of our story, we forget that reading and seeing are slightly different. You can't do one without the other, obviously, but sometimes the author can communicate things in a visual way without putting them in words.

For instance, I've used both CAPITALS when I wanted to capture the reader's attention and *italics* when presenting a book title. And you as the reader have assimilated these messages without my having to tell you.

There are many different ways to make your story visually interesting. For instance, you can set something apart by the use of indents (where the words are indented on both margins) so that it is noticeably different from the rest of the text. That's the technique used for the quotes throughout this book, and in novels it's handy for indicating the text of a letter or interior dialogue or a particular memory—indeed, just about anything that is in a different dimension or voice from the rest of the text around it.

You can also leave extra space between paragraphs. This usually indicates a change of scene or time, yet continues the subject. It isn't a major shift worthy of a chapter break, but it does say something has changed. Because the result is simply an extra empty line, the reader doesn't see anything, but in your manuscript, center the pounds sign (#) on that line so the typesetter knows to leave it blank. (I've used blank lines in this work to set off indented quotes and at the ends of sections to give the reader a visual break before the title of the next section.)

There's also the row of asterisks (* * * * *), which you can employ between two paragraphs to show a major change of time or direction, such as the end of a flashback when you want to bring the reader back to the present. These asterisks get set in type and warn the reader that there's a total shift of cast, time or subject.

Never hesitate to use commas, semicolons or dashes between phrases—particularly if they set off a complete idea—and even ellipses, those little dots that number three if it's just a pause (. . .) and four if it's the end of what could be a complete sentence that trails off at the end of a paragraph (. . . .).

If you aren't using the punctuation marks correctly, your style editor will let you know. And if you've overdone something . . . such as too many ellipses . . . your content editor will probably prod you to get rid of some of them.

Some authors make a fetish of page layouts or syntax stretching or punctuation ignoring, all of which can get tiresome very fast. Like the use of dialect, it runs the risk of becoming precious, self-conscious and distracting. That's not to say you shouldn't use it, just bring a thoughtful eye to it.

Several years ago Cormac McCarthy won the National Book Award and the National Book Critics Circle Award for *All the Pretty Horses*, which was a coming-of-age novel set right after World War II. Sometimes he has commas and sometimes not, but he never uses a quotation mark, and after a bit of confusion, the reader makes the adjustment. I don't know that that makes the work any stronger or weaker, but it is another example of an author using everything at his disposal.

One of the most important choices you'll make is which tense to use. Most authors stick with past perfect; it's safe, expected, easy to pick up or put down. At the other end of the spectrum is present tense, in which everything is happening right now, even as you hit the keyboard. Many people feel uncomfortable, either in writing or reading it, but once you get used to it, nothing else is as immediate.

In between are all sorts of personalized approaches to the subject. There are those who write in past tense but never slip into past perfect (he rode the horse 'til it dropped; he had ridden the horse 'til it had collapsed), and those who play back and forth with all of them for stylistic reasons.

When I first set out to do *Sierra*, I planned to follow five different families over a fifty-year period. The story evolves chronologically and while the focus of each interior section is written in past tense and centers on one family at a time, there are brief looks at what is happening to the other families during that same period. These segments are in present tense because everything is happening simultaneously, and they are quick vignettes, designed only to give balance rather than be deeply engaging. (It is a pattern I think the reader will respond to easily enough, though whether it will come out in print that way depends largely on how comfortable my editor and publisher are with it.)

In the Guinevere books there are occasional paragraphs that combine a mixture of tenses. These are the specific sequences containing the core of the legend, and I was playing off the time aspect of the "once and future king," as though these archetypical moments exist throughout the ages, separate from time and change. There were only a few in each book, usually set in italics and almost dreamlike in content, but no one ever questioned the technique and it did make it into print that way.

In his enormous American novel *Raintree County*, Ross Lockridge used stream of consciousness and a technique of slipping from past to present (or vice versa) that is immensely effective. Keeping the flashbacks and present material in separate chapters, he bridges the gap between them by running the last sentence of the first chapter directly on as the beginning sentence of the next chapter. Each half of the sentence makes different but complete sense in its own context, yet is also part of a different whole, just as your last waking thought slips into your first dreaming visual.

It's a technique that is at first startling, then intriguing—certainly one of the most interesting uses of combined tense and contents—and very powerful. (It was tempting to analyze *Raintree County* in this book, as it is quite a remarkable effort. But even though it was touted at its publication as the Great American Novel, the pretentiousness and verbosity make it a difficult read nowadays.

It is infinitely better than the movie, however, and well worth reading if you're truly interested in other people's use of the language.)

◆ ◆ ◆

Most all of the above has been garnered from reading, observing or talking with other authors—and, of course, my own experience. You will no doubt come up with your own array of concerns and discoveries, disasters and solutions pertinent to your specific work. That's what makes each writer unique.

In the meantime, the next chapter deals with generally mundane nuts and bolts of work habits and editing, both large and small, that will help your individual story achieve its own novel shape.

CHAPTER TEN

The Tools of Your Trade

E very so often someone asks, "When do you get your inspiration?" To which I generally reply, "When I open the utility bill."

Or to put it another way, "What do you do between inspirations?" "I pound out books on my computer."

Admittedly, being a historical novelist is not a run-of-the-mill job. But it is a profession that is fraught with its own special problems, including the need to get the concept from your head onto the paper WHETHER YOU FEEL LIKE IT OR NOT.

It is precisely this challenge, and the discipline required to meet it, that makes the difference between you and the hundreds of wanna-bes who have grand stories and interesting characters in mind but won't commit to treating writing like a job. It takes a combination of dedication, determination and desperation to become a historical novelist, and as with every other trade, the mastering of certain tools will make it easier.

REASONS OR EXCUSES?

If you're working on your first novel, you'll probably be supporting yourself in other ways, which makes writing all the more difficult. More than one hopeful author has worked on The Book every night after putting in an eight-hour day as a clerk, fast-food deliverer or temporary office employee, pounding away at the keyboard until the wee hours. Back in the 1950s Grace Metalious was raising a large family on a low income, keeping house and being a wife when she set out to write *Peyton Place*. It took years to complete her massive expose of life in a small town prior to World War II, and she wrote it by snatching a few minutes here or there in between all her other chores. The book went on to become a huge best-seller and spawned not only a movie but also a TV series.

Metalious's discipline should be an inspiration to all of us. Yet it's amazing how many would-be authors come up with reasons for why they can't/haven't/won't be able to complete their novels that sound pretty flimsy compared to the hurdles she overcame.

One of the most common excuses is, "I need a place to get away to for a month where I can write in peace."

I never hear that one without remembering all those promising young American novelists who wandered around Europe in the early 1930s—F. Scott Fitzgerald, Thomas Wolfe and Ernest Hemingway among them—each looking for the "right place" to work and each picking up and moving on in midsentence, convinced that some other spot would be more conducive to his muse. In the end they all finally discovered it is not where you are but how much you apply yourself that determines your output.

Granted, daily life is intrusive, demanding and not always conducive to pure inspiration and divine musings. If you can afford to retreat to some hidden spot and devote yourself entirely to your art, more power to you. But the amount of time working authors have to indulge in divine musings and pure inspiration is limited anyhow. And if you are really determined to get that manuscript finished, you'll let the aquarium go uncleaned for one more day, ignore the dustballs under the bed and turn down that invitation to party in order to sit down and *write*.

So the next time you're tempted to claim your book isn't finished because you haven't been able to get away from it all, stop and look at whether that's just an excuse to avoid the nitty-gritty work involved.

WORK HABITS

The patterns and hours of production vary tremendously from writer to writer. Some are faithful, almost religious, about addressing the blank page (or screen) every day. Most such people work in the morning, when they first get up and feel the mind is freshest.

Hemingway preferred to work in the early morning, often being up before dawn during his later years. When he'd completed the day's output, usually by midmorning, he was finished for the day and ready for partying, fishing, drinking or sporting as the season and his companions allowed. Thomas Wolfe, on the other hand, was prone to spending the evening getting ready to write but didn't really settle in to producing prose until somewhere around midnight, then worked straight through until dawn or later. And Margaret Mitchell seems to have put in regular office hours while her husband was at work. The important thing is, they did it *every day* (with the occasional break for Sundays and holidays) until the project was completed.

Sometimes you'll meet successful authors who never seem to work at all, always available to have a cup of coffee, go see a movie or dash off to the city for a weekend's adventure after which they disappear for a couple of weeks to work obsessively day and night, scribbling or typing away for ten, even fourteen, hours at a crack. In the end they've usually done as much as the everyday writer accomplishes in a month or two, but if they only do it once every four to six weeks, it all comes out in the wash.

The most important thing all these writers have in common is that they stick to the project until it's finished; how they get it done is purely a matter of what works best for each of them. And you'll do best if you do the same.

My system is to write new material through the day (sometimes morning, sometimes afternoon, sometimes both), then at the end of my work period I go back and make basic editing changes on the day's printout.

The next morning I begin by entering those changes in the computer, thereby priming the pump for the flow of new work that will begin as soon as I've gotten the editing taken care of. If the editing is so extensive as to need a whole rewrite, I tackle that once then move on. There will be plenty of time to polish it more fully when all the parts are in place.

KEEP GOING!

The second most important thing is to keep telling your story; do not give in to the desire to stop and perfect each segment before you tackle the next. It's amazing how many people get stuck in a particular chapter that they polish diligently for months but are never quite satisfied with. So they keep working at it, unable to let go until that piece is perfect.

That's a lot like painting by the numbers; you may get one corner of the picture just right, but you're nowhere near experiencing the flow and excitement of creation. It's far more important (and constructive) to get the entire tale down on paper, warts and all, *then* come back and refine it.

There are several reasons for this. Most readers want to be carried forward by the pull of the story and the interest they have in the characters. This means you need to keep your tale moving forward from peak to peak, following the arc of your story to climax and denouement in order to carry your audience along.

But it's next to impossible to move in that fine, free fashion if you can't focus on anything but one little segment. It may be a perfect jewel in and of itself, once you're finished, but that doesn't mean it fits into the rest of the fabric. So keep those words flowing, and worry about polishing individual chapters when they are part of a completed whole.

EDITING THE DAILY CATCH

Before the advent of videotape, movie directors used to watch hastily developed footage of yesterday's shoot the next morning to see if they needed to reshoot anything on that set. By the same token, your daily editing of the previous day's work will show you what you've got while it's still fresh enough that you can change it around without much trouble. In these sessions you're focusing on your most recent work, looking for the following:

Transparent Writing

This is the ideal most authors strive for, when the words are handled so smoothly they support the story without intruding, which lets the reader get totally involved and forget the very process of reading. Any time the language calls so much attention to itself that your reaction is to it instead of the story, it should be reined in immediately. You may opt to let it stay, but at least take a look at it.

That includes writing that's absolutely splendid, if it gets between you and the idea it's presenting. Michener slid into that, briefly, in *Hawaii*, with his description of a beautiful spot on Molokai, the island that was used as a leper colony and became a lawless pit, a hell on earth for its inhabitants. The contrast between the natural wonder and the human degradation is well made, but the writing about the beauty is so breathtaking, you end up being more conscious of it than the story.

Voice Changes

Watch for voice changes within a segment where the content of the story doesn't warrant it as a stylistic device. This usually happens when you've put different segments together that were written at different times with a different cadence.

For instance, I originally began the first Guinevere book, *Child of the Northern Spring*, as the bridal party was leaving Lake Windermere on the way south for Gwen to marry Arthur. But my editor wanted it to begin earlier, say, the night before, when Gwen tries to run away because she doesn't want to marry this new young king at all. So I wrote a new opening, and made the original one chapter two. Even though it isn't in the premier position, its first few pages still sound like an opening chapter; its pace, description and general formality all set it apart in a rather awkward way.

If you realize you have a sudden shift of tone or attitude which the story doesn't account for, rewrite the intruder so it flows along with the rest; you'll always regret it if it makes it into print and you can't go back and smooth that transition.

Murky Prose and Awkward Dialogue

These are two more things to clean up immediately. They can range from sentences that are so convoluted the reader loses track of what pronoun refers to which person to whole pages of dialogue in which no one is identified. This last is a style that, when it works, provides a kind of immediacy, but if you've ever had to go back and reread, mentally trying to keep track of which lines are said by who, you know how frustrating it can be.

A good wordsmith can handle that sort of dialogue when the content makes clear who is talking. For example, early on in *Sherwood* Parke Godwin has a scene where the Welshman, Will Scatloch, is giving young Robin lessons in the use of the bow.

> Shooting by instinct was the devil's own way until Robin learned to estimate distance without thinking in numbered paces. The draw was higher, anchored at the shooter's jaw rather than his shoulder. That took forever, it seemed, his aim getting worse, not better, but once he learned to *feel* the distance, his arrows were never far off the small targets—but never close enough for Will, of course.
>
> "There, Will. By Saint Wulfram, not a hand's width off."

"And no less, by Saint David."

"Well . . . close."

"Close for an Englishman."

"Well, what then?"

"You're only on it once, Robin. Feel it with the whole of you. Don't hurry." That was true enough. When Will shot, the draw, stance and loose were one fluid motion that only looked careless. "Be at the center, taking all the time you need."

"I did everything right, I swear."

"Right, is it?" Will pulled the errant shaft from the turf. "The deer of Sherwood stand yet in no peril."

Notice that you always know who is speaking, though each calls the other by name only once. (Although naming the listener in the speaker's dialogue is a way to keep the lines in the right character's mouth, those writers who do it in *every* sentence are clumsy indeed.)

Another thing to watch for in your editing are those places where you can weave in bits of business or color. Just as anachronisms are always lurking nearby, so are opportunities to further the painting of your world. For instance, Godwin's next passage begins after a double space, indicating a time lapse.

This September day he felt right. He paced away from the willow wand Will set upright in the meadow grass. As he paced, Robin listened to the first hint of autumn in the north wind—not cold yet, but you could feel it coming. The wind burned on his face, and Robin read its force, nocking the arrow as he walked.

"Far enough," Will commanded, distant behind him. "Mark your wind."

No need; he knew the wind sure as the shoes on his feet. Nevertheless, he plucked up a handful of grass and let it fall from shoulder height.

"Now!"

Robin turned in a smooth motion. The mild eyes went a little sharper as they found the target, as the body stanced, drew and loosed. The arrow sang through crisp September air—

Sure as a hawk stoops, swift as Da will fall on the Normans if they come. North wind all month, they'll never cross the Channel against it, and even if they do, there's Da and the king and every good lord and fyrd-man in England waiting for them. There, shaft, fly, stoop, and don't dare miss—

"Good, Rob!"

When he trotted back to Will, the little Welshman was kneeling by the arrow imbedded in the ground. The pile had driven in not a finger's width from the wand. Will's face creased with a broad grin. "Now the deer of Sherwood can beware of you."

This homey little sequence, which takes little more than a single page when set in type, gives you examples of smooth-moving dialogue, shows how Robin will become the finest archer in England, sets up the threat of Norman invasion via Robin's interior monologue in the italic portions and adds a further touch of the medieval world in the plucking of a handful of grass to check the wind— always a concern for an archer.

I do not know if Godwin added the touch of the grass later or included it in the first draft, but it's the kind of brushstroke you want to include to make the world you're creating all the more real for the reader.

Smoothness of Transitions

Does the sentence begin talking about one thing and end up examining another without a smooth bridge or direct flow of ideas? If so, this is the place and time to note it, either making the change now, or if you're too tired at the end of the day, jot "awkward" in the margin or "expand" or whatever will jog your memory so you can take care of it when you begin work next time.

Repetitions

You want to avoid having the same word or phrase show up several times on a page. Many people read slowly, hearing every phrase in their heads; as one reader said, she tells herself the story word by word. Such readers will likely come to a dead stop when the same word or phrase is repeated too often; it becomes a jarringly familiar note that makes them wonder if they've lost their place and are rereading what they just finished. Or else they'll conclude that your vocabulary is terribly limited and therefore your ideas probably are also. (This is assuming that you are not doing a stylistically intentional repeat. Those are a different matter and need to be done so strongly and persuasively, the reader recognizes early on what you're aiming for.)

When I encounter repetitions on the same page, I circle them, then either find a way to replace one of the words right then or address the matter next time I sit down to work, when my mind is fresh. You'll find that getting rid of repetitive words enlivens your prose considerably.

Inversions

More than one author has fumed that in first draft, everything from sentences to whole paragraphs seem to come out backward, so that the most important thought gets written at the beginning, and all the rest is explanation tagging along to shore it up.

I'm not sure why it's such a common problem, but seeing how often it's mentioned, it may be part of the creative process. Perhaps we're so intent on making our next point, we leap from one paragraph to the next, then have to back up and explain how we got there.

Remember that thread you're spinning? This is an example of keeping it smooth and unknotted so that each paragraph builds firmly to its conclusion and there's no reason for readers to feel you're doubling back on them.

You'll no doubt pick up other things in your daily editing. Each of us has our own quirks as to what needs to be avoided or corrected, so don't worry if your list is not the same as mine. Just remember that the reader wants to be transported by a compelling and dramatic story full of believable people in another time and place. How you work that magic is, in the long run, up to you.

MAJOR EDITING—ASSESSING WHAT YOU'VE GOT

It's a whale . . . it's a monster . . . it's super-manuscript! More than a few novelists have stood back and stared, aghast, at what they themselves have wrought. Margaret Mitchell was a smallish woman, and when seated on the sofa with the manuscript for *Gone With the Wind*, the stack of paper was as tall as she was. So don't feel that you've done something unheard of if you end up with what looks and feels like a huge and cumbersome behemoth.

I think it was Michelangelo who said every statue was just resting inside its block of marble; it was the sculptor's job to chip away the excess until the trapped masterpiece was exposed. One might say that major editing is looking for and at the masterpiece you've created but not yet fully exposed.

Overall editing requires that you sit down and read your manuscript straight through from the beginning. This can be at any time; Hemingway was said to begin each day's work on his first novel by reading the entire manuscript from the beginning. Other authors don't read the whole thing until they've completed the telling for the first time. And according to a few jaded editors, some of the lazier ones never even do that.

During this editing you must look at *everything*—from silly blunders to what's left out; from pesky anachronisms to overall questions of repetitions, foreshadowing, opening scenes and pace, to say nothing of consistency. (Editing a completed manuscript is the ultimate juggling act because you need to keep everything in mind constantly. It's both exciting and exasperating, and many of us love and hate it at one and the same time!)

OOPS!

Just as words often get repeated in first-draft writing, duplicate scenes have been known to creep in when you weren't looking or show up in several different places when you sit down and do a complete read-through.

Sometimes this comes about because of sloppy cut-and-paste work on the computer, where you copy a sequence from one file to another but forget to delete it in its original placement. And sometimes you simply forget that you've already taken care of this particular matter earlier and so write it out a second time later on.

(Here's an example where sticking to the 3″ × 5″ carding process helps; just put a check in the corner of each card when that scene is completed, and move the card to the used stack. It won't catch every repeat because the human mind is fertile and easily distracted, and books take months, sometimes even years, to complete, so it's hard to keep every detail in mind all the time, but the cards do help.)

Repetition of the same material will slow down your story, even if the words and telling are different. Unless there's a particular reason to present it from another point of view, such repetitions can make agents, editors or publishers discard the whole thing.

FORESHADOWING

Foreshadowing is the fine art of planting an idea in the reader's mind well before it's time to have it meet the needs of the story. As the name implies, it is only a hint of what is to come—not so important as to stop the reader cold, but enough to lay the foundation for future events. If you compare writing a novel to stringing beads on a necklace, foreshadowing is the first introduction of a particular color that isn't being focused on yet.

Frequently foreshadowing is built in as you go along. Remember that wind that Robin was checking during the archery lesson in *Sherwood?* A September wind, out of the north, presaging autumn, burning against his face. "He knew the wind sure as the shoes on his feet. . . . North wind all month, they'll never cross the Channel against it."

The reader absorbs all that as ambiance, color, simply part of Robin's world. But less than three pages later chapter two begins:

> Throughout August and well into September, Duke William's armada waited at Dives for a south wind that perversely refused to blow. Vanes pointed north day after day while good campaigning weather wasted away.

Now the reader realizes that that wind is far more than a colorful touch; it's actually controlling the destinies of the men who are watching it, including William of Normandy who is having a hard time holding his troops in readiness to invade England.

In the next three pages Godwin sets up William's predicament, his self-doubts contrasting with his ability to control his men, if not the weather. He's a man we can admire and understand. Then suddenly Godwin slides in a simple sentence:

> William's nose caught the change before his eye.
>
> The air—the smell was different. Dryer, warmer. He glanced at the weathervane, hardly daring to hope. The vane quivered and swung around to point firmly and at last south. The Duke took a deep, sufficing breath of the quickening breeze.
>
> Yes. Now. By God's face, *now.* His voice carried far along the beach to other men who smelled the change and knew what it could mean. "The wind! Look! God *is* with us. To ship! We *go!*"

Thus we're swept along with the excitement of William's conquest of England without even realizing we were thoroughly and carefully set up. That's an excellent example of how a good writer can build a little subtle foreshadowing into a pivotal turning point down the line.

Sometimes, however, you don't even know you need to foreshadow something until you're part way through the manuscript and realize you forgot to lay the proper foundation for the next plot twist. Or something unexpected and wonderful happens, but there's been nothing to prepare the reader for it. So you go back and find a place to mention it earlier in the text.

For instance, when Percival came to Camelot I needed something that would immediately establish him as the "wild child." Growing up in the woods, without benefit of civilization, he comes into Arthur's court full of wonder and savagery—never been in a house before, never learned any manners or social behavior. All he knows is that Arthur's men ride splendid horses and are beautifully equipped. In the traditional version he inquires if they are angels, so brightly does he think they shine.

I saw him advancing across the Great Hall, garbed in nothing but skins and tatters and superalert. Suddenly his eye falls on a falcon resting on a perch next to its owner. Quick as a flash Percival slips a stone into his sling, and with a flick of his wrist, drops the bird dead. Pouncing on it, he wrings its neck for good measure and presents it to Guinevere for the stewpot while the rest of the knights gasp in disbelief.

It was a great scene, full of color and character—except that until that moment no one at the Round Table had even heard of falconry. (It wasn't really taken up in Britain until after the Crusades, some five hundred years later, when the English knights returned from the Middle East with falcons on their wrists.)

But because my Palomides had already gone on a quest looking for his roots among the Arab tribes in Palestine, it wasn't hard to go back and include a falcon among the treasures he brought back with him. It not only added color to Palomides (traditionally the exotic outsider whom everyone respects), it also provided the perfect foil to show Percival's untamed nature later.

Mystery writers are forever foreshadowing things that are later developed both as real clues and as red herrings. Since the mystery fan is watching for them, they tend to be presented more fully when first introduced. In most stories, however, the first encounter should be low-keyed, a natural part of the tale, but more a touch of color than an actual theme. There's a reason for this, and it has to do with human nature.

The mind is a sponge. It retains all sorts of things and sometimes stores them almost verbatim. Therefore the best storyteller is careful not to lay out an idea too fully in foreshadowing, lest the reader, encountering it later on, says, "but I already knew that," and puts the book down, bored.

So how do you determine what is enough foreshadowing and not too much? Again it comes down to the writer constantly making choices. In the case of the falcon there wasn't much chance of getting trapped; the bird was a bit of exotica when first encountered and the object of an uncivilized act when dispatched. If there had been any reason to play up the relationship between Percival and Palomides, I might have reintroduced the bird midway between the first sight and its demise: someone wanting to buy it from Palomides, for instance, and his being adamant about how special it is to him. That would, of course, heighten the reader's reaction when Percival does it in, and make hostility on Palomides' part that much more likely.

Another way to handle foreshadowing is to come at it from two different points of view; that is, have several characters mention it at different times, perhaps displaying different attitudes toward it. But however you do it, *always* make sure that each mention provides something new the readers haven't been told before so that it piques their interest and sets them up for the fulfillment of the subject whenever that comes about.

PACING YOUR WORDS

Although I wouldn't presume to tell you what or what not to do by way of sequencing, the pace at which you do it may be crucial to your sale, and there are some tricks of the trade you can build in as you tell your story.

Pace is a relative thing; get the readers hooked, make them care about a character or an event and they'll hang in through the slow and thoughtful as well as slam-bang action. So try to present something both unusual and universal right from the beginning, as William Shaara does in the opening of *The Killer Angels.*

THE SPY

He rode into the dark of the woods and dismounted. He crawled upward on his belly over cool rocks out into the sunlight, and suddenly he was in the open and he could see for miles, and there was the whole vast army below him, filling the valley like a smoking river. It came out of a blue rainstorm in the east and overflowed the narrow valley road, coiling along a stream, narrowing and choking a white bridge.

In less than a paragraph Shaara has involved us in the situation, the danger (spying) playing off the beauty of the scene; surprise at the size of the enemy army; the weather; the stream and bridge below. We're there, caught up immediately in the scene, and the fact that it takes four more pages before we come to the first dialogue with another human doesn't matter; the pace is enlivened by our interest.

Cutting

Another way to control pace is by cutting. Many new novelists, having fallen in love with words, spell out everything their characters do, taking them step-by-step through each day, which slows things down considerably. The first time I recognized how to specifically speed things up came in the second Guinevere book when she learns from one of Tristan's students that the Cornish harper is being called home to his Uncle's court.

> The boy's discouragement (at losing his teacher) was almost tangible, so I said I'd see what could be arranged and turned my attention to the spice cupboard, wondering why Mark wanted Tristan to come home.
>
> "It seems that after all these years of searching, the King of Cornwall has found a royal family who will give him a child-bride."
>
> Dinadan's announcement took us all by surprise. Mark was a walking monument to self-indulgence.

This technique of introducing a question then following it immediately with the answer allows you to move from midday in the kitchen to that evening in the hall, or even several days later, if your story unfolds that way. The thing to remember is that the thread of interest and theme become a bridge over time, and as long as the subject is kept firmly in front of the reader, you can swing over endless swamps of daily and mundane activity.

Hooks

These also keep up the pace because they pique the readers' interest and get them to keep reading. They can be used right from the beginning (as Ken Kesey does in *Sometimes a Great Notion*, which we'll look at in the next chapter), be sprinkled judiciously throughout the book or employed effectively at the ends of chapters.

In the latter case they usually take the form of an idea, question or suggestion that makes the reader want to start the next chapter just to see how the matter gets resolved.

(end of chapter two)
With that in mind, he set out to confront the king.
(beginning of chapter three)
"You must be mad!" His Highness slammed the tankard down and turned a red-rimmed eye on the hapless messenger.

Carries the readers right along, doesn't it? And gets them into the next chapter as well. (I personally prefer short chapters—between ten and twenty manuscript pages, max—because as a reader I'll check out the length of the next chapter, and if it's only a few pages, will put off making phone calls, doing the dishes or paying bills in order to read just one more section. You can figure whatever works to keep you hooked will also work on your readers.)

One last word on pace: Give your readers a break now and then—a resolution, secession of pressure, a few pages of hope and happiness. Not only does it allow them a chance to savor your story and people, it also keeps both you and them from burning out. And remember, you are writing a historical, not a high-tech thriller or modern horror book, so you don't have to keep the decibels pounding.

RESOLVING YOUR CONFLICT

The climax of a book is the high point of its arc, the thing toward which you, the characters and the reader have all been moving, willingly or not, since the first paragraph. Depending on your story line and the role of history in your plot, the climax can take various forms and may include confrontation, revelation or explanation.

For instance, the climax of *Moby Dick* is confrontation in the classic sense with Captain Ahab and his great white nemesis going down to the depths together, whereas the climax of *Gone With the Wind* is the revelation for Scarlett that Ashley is more dream than reality, and it is Rhett whom she loves, wants and needs. Sometimes, as in a biographical novel, it is death that ends the story, and then the author turns to whatever explanation or evaluation seems most reasonable or poignant.

When you're writing, editing and rewriting your climax, don't hesitate to pull out all the stops. This is the cathartic moment, the apex of the story, so make it as intense as possible, still keeping to the color and mood of your piece. Remember that it's easier to tone a thing down in later editing than it is to ramp it up, so don't hold back here.

Also, you'll probably want to bring your reader back down to earth with a sense of completion; some novelists simply drive the point home and leave it at that, but as in lovemaking, it's much more satisfying to have a little pillow talk afterward. That's what the denouement is—those last couple of paragraphs or pages that round out and finish things off. For instance, Scarlett's inner dialogue about returning to Tara is the denouement of Mitchell's book, and it is right in keeping with the personality of the protagonist. Hemingway's ending of *Farewell to Arms*, where his protagonist walks back to the hotel from the hospital—and notes the rain—is equally appropriate for that work. Both authors sustain the mood of the characters and eras right to the last sentence, while wrapping up the story enough so that the reader feels really satisfied.

Larry McMurtry's *Lonesome Dove* has a kind of prolonged denouement, depending on whether you see the climax as Gus's death or Call's taking the body back from Montana to Texas in order to bury it in the spot Gus has requested. Call's morbid journey provides a kind of reprise and curtain call for each of the major characters built up during the onset of the book, but the last scenes, when Call himself isn't sure if he's dead or alive as he returns to the burned out saloon in Lonesome Dove, are tremendously powerful.

IS IT DONE YET?

Well now, looks as though you've actually written a book! Like a mother having just given birth, a hen cackling over laying an egg or God smiling because creation was good, you're probably on one of the grandest highs you'll ever know. And rightly so; not many people actually FINISH the novels they always think they're going to write. After all, you've gotten your whole story on paper, read it from cover to cover and filled the margins with notes and comments, arrows, cryptic messages and all the rest of the hen scratching that is actually each author's personal shorthand to herself. Surely the end is in sight. Isn't it?

Well, yes and no. Like Michelangelo, you've gotten the excess marble chipped away. But there's still refining, rewriting and preparing your manuscript to be viewed by others. Sometimes that takes only a little while, and sometimes it takes weeks or even months, particularly if you do much restructuring or rewriting. So polish up your patience, your finest chisel and your best eye for drama and form because the next step is making it all as smooth as possible.

CHAPTER ELEVEN

The Mark of a Professional

T he best fiction reads effortlessly, as though the story simply tells itself. But often an immense amount of time, consideration and just plain brain-racking went into the refining, rewriting, cutting and polishing necessary to achieve those results.

Kenn Davis, a painter who has published some dozen mystery novels, summed it up for all of us when he said, "I'm not a writer, I'm a rewriter."

Dull as that may sound, it's the difference between the enthusiastic amateur and the true professional.

REWRITING

As a young author I was convinced that the first draft was the one with the "juice"; anything else was watered down and somehow weaker. And sometimes that's true—the first draft is the one with the most spontaneity and often remains the most exciting for the author.

But over the years I've seen other authors' work in various drafts and realize that some truly splendid fiction began as a handful of gravel containing, here and there, a few nuggets of genuine gold. A good novel is a work of art, not just an uneven patchwork of sketches, and if you are not willing to go through and polish, balance and adjust your work into a viable whole, if you're only interested in the creative excitement of getting it on paper for the first time, you need to view your writing as a hobby, not a profession.

There is nothing wrong with that, but if you're thinking in terms of getting published, you'll learn to accept, and maybe even enjoy, rewriting, for there's usually much of it needed to achieve the best result.

Many authors find they are either too fat or too lean in the first draft. Because I'm an extremely verbal person and lyric by nature, I'm forever going back and "putting teeth" into my prose. (Artist's paper is referred to as having a tooth if it's rough enough to hold pigment for a picture; slick paper just lets the pencil, pastel or charcoal glide over the surface.) In much the same way, my native slickness can lull people to sleep, so for a book like *Sierra* I correct it by taking out extra words, shortening sentences and getting as much punch as possible out of each line.

Other authors have just the opposite problem, writing with a spareness that leaves nothing but the bones of the story clacking together. For them rewriting is a matter of fleshing out feelings, surroundings and characters.

You may find that your most deviling problem is a lack of focus, so in rewrite you'll be watching for places where you've directed the reader's attention to a scatter of different things (what one author calls the "jerky camera" syndrome) rather than homing in on the heart of the drama. Again, these are very specific aspects of your own style, and you are the only one who can perfect it. Remember that the most important thing is to ALWAYS KEEP THE ARC OF THE STORY AND ITS PACE IN MIND, and do your rewriting accordingly.

THE CUTTING ROOM FLOOR

No matter how much you love your little darlings, you have to be willing to kill 'em off when necessary. This is true whether it's a scene or a character or a theme that's become a diversion; if it interferes with the balance and pace of the overall book, out it goes, no matter how good the writing or how charming the sequence or person. Put that ham back in a supporting role, stash the historical asides in your glossary (if you're following McCullough's model) and be willing to condense four pages of witty but superfluous dialogue to a single sentence—"We decided to go by way of the Volga River."—when necessary.

There are two critical questions you should always ask, both in editing and rewriting: "What is the purpose of this scene?" and "Is there a better way to get that information across?" This is particularly true when you come across something that just doesn't seem to fit in.

If a scene is jarring but the content is good, you may find it's misplaced and will become more powerful if you change the sequence. Or maybe it can be brought out with greater power or economy in another way, perhaps seen from someone else's point of view.

Yet no matter how many things you try (or how much time you spend on it), there're going to be some sequences that end up on the cutting room floor, either through your own sense about the book's arc or your editor's prodding. Often even wonderful scenes and writing get excised from the final manuscript.

Don't feel bad about it. I regularly write at least twice as much as actually makes it between the covers of a book; whole scenes, subplots and extra characters get relegated to a box of printouts and computer limbo. But while it's occasionally frustrating to have to eliminate something I'm really proud of, I don't look on that writing as having been a waste of time. My contention has always been that while the reader doesn't need to know such and such, you as the author obviously did or you wouldn't have written it out. Yes, these scenes happened, but just because I lived through the sequence with the characters doesn't mean the reader needs to. (Only twice in all my years of writing have I gotten into a scene and said, "No, these characters wouldn't say or do that.")

So ALWAYS KEEP THE ARC OF THE STORY AND ITS PACE IN MIND, and give up whatever gets in the way.

OPENING SCENES

Now that you've got the first draft finished and can look at your book as a whole, this is the time to go back and reassess your opening scenes.

It's estimated that the customer in a bookstore will browse the first three pages and if not hooked by them, will put the book down and go on to buy a different one. Agents, editors and critics generally give a manuscript fifty pages or so before passing their verdicts, which gives you a little more leeway. But everyone knows those first few pages are terribly important and thus will be paying close attention to them.

Often the best opening gambit isn't where we, as authors, think it will be, and more than one novelist has either had to cut out whole sequences to get to the most interesting opening scene or been asked to go back and write in a chapter or two so as to bring the reader up to speed.

Sometimes we're simply too close to the project to see what works best. Remember, that opening scene is crucial, both because it sets the tone of the book and (hopefully) captures the reader's interest, so those pages need to be good. Some are more successful than others, obviously, and most of us agonize over them, whether it's our first novel or our tenth.

For instance, Margaret Mitchell was *not* happy with the opening of *Gone With the Wind.* She rewrote it many times and settled on the picnic at Twelve Oaks as much because she ran out of time as because it was her favorite. It does get the idea across, however: Scarlett is seen in all her flirtatious glory, the Civil War begins and the reader is introduced both to the unattainable Ashley and the rakish Rhett.

Colleen McCullough's *The Thorn Birds* begins with one of the most poignant and terrifying scenes I've ever read. While it doesn't involve physical violence on the little girl Meggie, one's heart breaks for her as the first and only beautiful thing she's known— a doll surreptitiously given her for her fourth birthday—is savagely torn apart by her older brothers.

With that scene McCullough establishes the harshness of life, the fragility of love and beauty and the vulnerability of Meggie, all of which are themes that play out in this novel of early twentieth-century Australia. That's exactly what you want the first scene to do: establish a voice, mood, characters, location or theme in such a way as to hook the audience into reading more.

Occasionally a great opening scene throws down a challenge, as in Ken Kesey's *Sometimes a Great Notion.* After a poetic page that sets the scene in the shaggy Oregon Coast Range on a windy, drizzly day, the reader's attention is drawn to an ancient two-story house perched on the river's edge across the water from the road, where a dismembered arm dangles inexplicably from a fir pole projecting out of a second-floor window. The oozing, dripping thing twists and turns over the water as a pack of dogs whimper and bark and circle on the bank, unable to reach it. On the far side of the river a crowd gathers to stare at the grotesque scene, calling over and over the name of the house's occupant, but no one comes out to explain.

Indeed, neither does the author, who presents most of the story before the puzzle is solved. More than once I would have put the book down unfinished if it weren't for the nagging question of that singular arm on the opening page. I have no idea how many times Kesey wrote or rewrote that first scene, or where it originally came in his first draft, but the final result is very, very powerful.

Remember that the reader will assume the opening scene is typical of the whole book. You wouldn't put a soft, romantic sequence at the start of an action thriller for instance, as the customer who scans and buys it for the romance will feel cheated, and the action thriller reader won't bother reading past page one. Therefore you'd do well to make your openings consistent with the mood and feel of the rest of the book.

In my Guinevere trilogy the first volume, *Child of the Northern Spring*, dealt with Gwen's childhood, so it begins with a young girl's exuberance:

> I, Guinevere, Celtic Princess of Rheged and only child of King Leodegrance, woke to a clatter of activity in the stable-yard. The sound of gruff orders and jingling harnesses was accompanied by swearing and grunting and the occasional stomp of a large, impatient hoof.
>
> I scrambled out of bed and ran to the window. Sure enough, down by the barns the yard was filling with people and animals. Arthur's men were strapping packframes on the ponies, and before long even the traveling horses would be saddled.
>
> Too soon tomorrow had arrived, and a surge of panic rose up to choke me.

Volume two explores the political background and basis for Arthur's developing the Round Table and traces the growth of the legendary court, Gwen and Arthur's marriage and a number of the love stories of the legend. It originally opened with Gwen listening to her mother-in-law's explanation of Arthur's origins, as the old woman lies dying in a convent. But during the writing, it occurred to me that Gwen's sitting in a cold stone cell was (1) too dramatic an introduction of the book that would follow and (2) an excellent way to hook the reader into the drama of book three. Therefore, in a much lighter vein, *Queen of the Summer Stars* begins as follows:

> I, Guinevere, wife of King Arthur and High Queen of Britain, dashed around the corner of the chicken coop, arms

flying, war-whoop filling my throat. The children of the Court were ranged behind me, shouting gleefully as a half-grown piglet skittered across the [muddy] courtyard of the Mansion . . . . [She throws herself on the pig—which gets away—then looks up] to find a small, mud-spattered priest staring down at me in astonishment.

"Your Highness?"

I grinned at the tentative greeting and scrambled back to my feet. Heaven knows what he expected of his High King's wife, but I was what he got.

That single scene establishes Gwen as independent, humorous and in no way self-impressed. But for the Prologue to *Guinevere: the Legend in Autumn*, it was time to go back to the bare cell, not in a convent this time, but a prison.

I, Guinevere, High Queen of Britain and wife to King Arthur, sat in the shadows of the stone cell and stared into the brazier. A layer of soft gray ash blanketed the embers until a charred branch collapsed onto them and the molten heart of the coals flared up. I gasped and, shivering violently, turned to face the bed . . . by now both my feet and legs ached with the cold.

No mind—the dawn will bring heat enough. Heat and flames and swirling smoke around the stake . . .

You'll notice that Gwen's interior thoughts are set off by italics—an example of playing with texture. Also, her sense of who she is changes from Celtic princess and only child to proud new wife and incidentally High Queen at the beginning of book two, then High Queen and also wife of Arthur in book three, when her duties and responsibilities have become as important as her personal relationships.

I happen to like the symmetry of framing a book with Prologue and Epilogue, though some authors use only one or the other, and most ignore them entirely. It can be a good way to establish relationships, location, mood or character without having to go into depth, and you can drop in hooks to catch the reader without unbalancing the actual flow of the story.

MAKING THE MOST OF THE MOMENT

Rewriting also means recognizing the opportunities that almost slipped away unnoticed. Remember that for the most part you want to have your characters act out the story; the reader wants to experience it, not read a report of it. So now's the time to mine your research notes and folders, as well as rack your brain for chances to use both historical events and your personal characters in ways that further your story. (By now you should know both your people and your era well enough to feel comfortable with their integration.)

For instance, Margaret Mitchell was playing to the high drama of Atlanta going up in flames when she had Rhett guide Scarlett through the burning streets. Not only were there exploding buildings and falling storefronts all around, there was the shock of discovering that it was the Confederate army that set it all ablaze, wanting to deny the Union forces the use of equipment or ammunition.

A tense time, right? And what does Rhett do, once they reach the outskirts of the city? He makes sure Scarlett is on the road to Tara, then leaves to go fight for the obviously lost cause of the Confederacy! In that one moment Mitchell shows us an unexpected sentiment behind Rhett's sophisticated opportunism, implies that he has every confidence that Scarlett can take care of herself and adds the potential of his being killed to the already high-stakes brew.

Now that's making the most of your material!

STICKING TO THE POINT

Several years ago there was a remarkable film made on the life of Beethoven. The actors were excellent, the dialogue mostly believable, art direction and photography very evocative of the era. Even the premise was interesting: Who had been the great love of the composer's life, and why was he so determined to get, and keep, custody of his nephew?

Unfortunately something happened between the conception of the idea and the final product: the pace was uneven, the transitions were often too abrupt and the story line wandered, looped, snarled and threatened to disappear entirely on numerous occasions. That can happen in a novel as well, what with diversions, historical fascinations or lack of a firm hand in editing and rewriting.

Always keep the arc of the story and its pace in mind, and tell your tale through as clearly as possible.

HALF-SCENES

If your pace is flagging, you may find that half-scenes are the solution. You can use them in rewriting either to add points you'd forgotten earlier—even foreshadowing—or to get across the information from a deleted sequence and still keep the pace moving.

Half-scenes are the literary equivalent of the little scenes performed in many Shakespearean productions in front of a closed curtain while the stagehands rearrange the set. They are sketches that go to the heart of the matter, involve information rather than important action or emotions and can be life-savers when your book gets too long.

With a half-scene you don't need to go into detail, give the actors' names or backgrounds or build to a climax in the scene. Just bring them on stage and let them pass on the information, usually in dialogue, which both furthers the plot and keeps the pace up. It can be as short as just a couple of lines or as long as the following example from *Sierra*, when I wanted to capture the ferment of San Francisco during the autumn of 1849.

> Leaving his horse at a stable, Danny climbed the hill to the Post Office where a crowd of people milled in front of the none-too-steady building though the mail boat wasn't expected for another week.
>
> "I wouldn't hold your breath if I were you, sonny," a crusty prospector said. "It's going on three months since we seen the last one. When that steamer does come puffing up, wheweee, this here little gathering won't look like nothin'."
>
> Danny stared around at the fifty or more men, and thought it looked like something to him. Most of them came from the mines—scruffy, dirty fellows, some full of boasts, some downcast and sheepish—and some were the minions of local business men sent to post letters and orders when the postmaster opened the window for an hour each day. But the fellow next to him turned out to be a journalist from England who regaled Danny with tales of his travels, then lowered his voice as the subject grew darker.
>
> "Seen some heartbreaking things as well," he confided.

"Young men so wasted they look to be closer to eighty than twenty. They're all over . . . curled up in alleys, begging on street-corners, or too sick and broken by the mines to work for a living here, too broke and hopeless to earn their way home. Dying like flies . . . suicide, despair, lack of doctoring. Sometimes you hear 'em at night, sobbing out the last of their lives or muttering over a bottle in the shadow of someone else's shelter . . . find 'em dead in the morning, drag 'em off to potter's field. No city's healthy to live in, but this is the hardest yet."

Danny nodded, sobered and shocked by such an idea. It was one thing to die alone, pitting yourself against the elements in the wilds of the Sierra, something else to turn up your toes in a place so full to bursting with other humans.

"It's those damn ruffians pretending to be policemen," someone else said. "They get up in their uniforms and parade through the streets on Sundays, terrorizing every [one] in sight . . . Now they're harassing us store-owners, saying we need to buy protection. What we need is an honest to goodness police force."

"Won't do no good without a jail."

"Someone's got to clean up the town."

"Not *too* clean."

That brought a ripple of laughter and everyone looked to see who'd spoken. A laconic young man moved his cud of tobacco to the other cheek and began to philosophize. "You let that kind of thinking loose, next thing you know they'll be closing down the houses. Take away the gambling hells and whores, a man's got nothing left to do in 'Frisco."

There was much nodding of agreement as the post master opened the shutters and the line began to inch past the window. The British journalist turned to Danny. "You explored the fleshpots yet?"

When Danny shook his head, the reporter grinned. "You've a treat in store. There's plenty to choose from. . . ."

That's about average length for a half-scene. Figuring three printed pages for every five of manuscript, it will print out at a little more than a single page and covers the polyglot population, boredom, sickness and despair, the focus on gambling and whoring and the constant threat of anarchy, all of which were the major components of that city at that time.

The English journalist, by the way, is patterned on a real fellow who wrote extensively both about life in the Mother Lode in 1849 and San Francisco. I thought of giving his name but then ran into two common considerations for historical novelists: Do you put your own dialogue in a historical person's mouth (some authors do, some don't); and does the reader need to know specifically who this character is—will he show up again (no), will the name ring a bell (only for scholars) and does it further the drama to identify him (no)? So I used him anonymously in a half-scene and got the information across that way.

Some half-scenes are shorter, and occasionally you'll run into one that's longer, though pretty soon that verges on a whole scene. At any rate, keep it in mind as a solution when you need to get rid of a longer segment that slows down the pace.

TYING UP THOSE LOOSE ENDS

Charles Dickens wrote most of his novels for serialization in British magazines (some of which he owned), and occasionally he'd barely complete the next installment in time to give it to the typesetter. This meant there was little time for rewriting, reediting and all the luxuries we so much take for granted in the late twentieth century with the help of computers.

Since most of us are not latter-day Dickenses and don't have the excuse of a magazine's deadline, we have to keep a weather eye out for loose ends. Goals need to be reached, conflicts resolved and the reader satisfied that all are accounted for, one way or another. So it's worthwhile to take the time, now while you're doing your rewriting, to get all those loose ends tidied up.

One of those loose ends is the simple and basic question, Now that you have your story down on paper, does it work? You've cried with your characters, sweated with and for them, smiled from ear to ear when something wonderful happened, but will anyone else? Is the resolution as cathartic for others as it was for you? Are your characters memorable, your setting evocative, your pace satisfactory for the outside reader? Will anyone else besides you *want* to read it? And how do you find out?

Since family are unlikely to give you a truly unbiased reaction, this is the time to turn to literate friends, history or literature teachers or some form of writing workshop, conference or any other group that can give you some objective feedback. They may not be able to help you fix your problems, but you'll at least get a yes or no reaction. When I gave the opening chapter of my first novel to a good friend to read, it put her to sleep within three pages. Obviously I needed to reexamine what I'd done, and on dissecting it, it was clear I'd been reporting page after page of background instead of jumping right into some engrossing action.

FRIENDLY FIRE

People often ask what I think of writers groups that meet for the sole purpose of reading and "critting" each other's work. It's the kind of thing that is great if it works and can be a real demoralizer if it doesn't.

Some groups last for decades and the members grow to trust each other implicitly, thereby providing wonderful feedback, encouragement and support. When it works that way, it's great. But if you find you're getting more criticism than support, with other people being clever at your expense, or wanting to take the story away from you and tell it *their* ways, you're wasting time that could be spent working on the next chapter (or looking for an agent). Therefore I suggest that you test those waters for yourself and decide based on the merits of your own feelings.

More experienced authors often caution a newcomer not to talk his story away. More than one hopeful has found he's told the tale so often to so many friends and relations, the juice has gone out of it by the time he starts to put it on paper. It's a point you might want to heed.

On the other hand, if you have a writer friend, companion or mentor who is truly interested, objective and (we should all be so lucky) involved in the industry as well, by all means share with that person. Some authors enjoy discussing difficult problems, sharing large sections of current work and giving each other the benefit of an immediate response, good or bad. If they can tell you what pleased and excited them as well as what confused or put them to sleep, they will be of value to you. If all they can do is carp on the things they think are "wrong," they certainly aren't being helpful.

In the long run, it's all pretty much for you to decide, and if you find a supportive friend or group, thank your lucky stars and listen to the feedback. Otherwise remember that most authors work alone, and the professional writer isn't going to care if the Thursday Night Scribblers think her work is good or bad.

PREPPING YOUR MANUSCRIPT

My husband used to say, "Never show a fool a half-finished job," which is excellent advice in any endeavor. Certainly it applies to the professionals in the publishing world because while they may not be fools, you're asking for trouble if you send them anything but the very best and most professional product you can muster. In other words, NEVER SEND OUT A ROUGH DRAFT unless the agent or editor has been begging on bended knee, and even then you're probably shooting yourself in the foot.

There are a number of reasons for this: Agents and editors are busy people, having lots of other manuscripts to read, including those of their moneymaking clients. An agent can't be expected to be an editor, and an editor wants to tell you how to improve your book, not how to write it to begin with. Neither of them wants to spend time deciding which draft to use (that, after all, is what *writers* do). Not only is it neither the agent's nor the editor's cup of tea, but the agent may get bored with the project and decline to handle it at all; writers don't mind going over and over the same story from many viewpoints, but if agents enjoyed doing that, they'd be writing, instead of selling, books.

So even before you start looking for an agent—which deserves (and gets) a chapter in itself—make sure you have a completed, polished and fully prepped manuscript printed out and ready to send.

Since this is a book on constructing historical fiction and not on the use of style, grammar or other basics, I suggest you get one of the excellent books on those subjects if they are giving you trouble. You'll save yourself—and your style editor—a good deal of misery, and it may mean the difference between a sale and a rejection.

In the meantime, all agents appreciate certain niceties in the presentation of a manuscript, such as:

Clear, Clean Pages, easy to read and devoid of hand-scribbles. With the advent of PCs and their attendant printers, there's no excuse for the old-fashioned hand-corrections that used to be scattered throughout typed manuscripts. Remember, both agents and editors spend many hours every day reading, so anything you can do to make that job easier is going to be to your advantage.

Spelling and Grammar loom large as problem areas these days. There are times when even the most patient of agents will put aside a well-told tale because the author hasn't bothered to learn the rudiments of our language. How you use that language to say what you want is a matter of taste, talent and individual expression; spelling and the basics of punctuation and grammar are not. Presenting a professional with a manuscript full of misspelled words and nonexistent or misleading punctuation is a serious mistake.

At the very least, if you've got a computer, use its spelling program to check your whole manuscript; it takes a lot of the dog work out of the job and assures a more polished product. Be alert for homonyms, however—their/there, it's/its, our/hour and so forth. These slide through the cracks just as typos slip into galleys, and there's nothing for it but to be on the lookout every time you reread your work.

The actual format for manuscripts is pretty basic, and while some ask for this and others that, the following has worked well for me.

Header goes across the top of the page. Approximately one-half inch from the top, it should have your book title and name in the left corner and page number on the outside edge of the right-hand corner.

SIERRA/Persia Woolley   Ch. L13, Donner Party 1/23/96 125

Start First Pages of chapters between one-third and one-half of the way down the page. This leaves plenty of room for art directors, style editors and everyone else to make notes relative to type style, spacing, ornaments or anything else of consequence.

Double-Space your text, and remember that Courier 12 is one of the easiest of fonts to read. Most professionals won't read a manuscript with type smaller than 10 points, and it's certainly more thoughtful to use 12-point type. *Don't* go in for fancy fonts to show how creative you are; it is not only amateurish, it may make the agent or editor cross if there's any problem in reading it.

Number Your Pages Consecutively. It sounds self-evident, I know, but every so often a wanna-be complains, "Every chapter begins at page one because each one is a new file, and I don't know how to make my computer change." Either learn more about your computer, have a computer-literate friend adjust it for you or leave off the printed numbers and handwrite the number on each page. Not only do publishers calculate how many words they're dealing with on the basis of number of pages, they also figure how much paper, what kind of binding and other cost-related factors that go into publishing a book, all of which affects their decision as to how much to offer for your manuscript.

Margins on a manuscript are traditionally an inch or inch and a half at top and bottom, though I've seen pages that started higher and ended closer to the bottom of the paper. Side margins should be big enough to put notes in. I personally like an inch on the right-hand side and and inch and a half on the left, precisely for notes and comments. Then, too, I keep my manuscript pages in a three-ring binder, so I need plenty of space on the left side for the ring holes. NEVER justify the right-hand margin, as that establishes false spacing and makes the word count difficult.

Copy Your Work, or ask your printer to spit out another whole manuscript. We've come a long way from the days of an original and one carbon copy, and there's absolutely no reason for not having a backup hard copy in case you need it. (The traditional excuse of the aspiring writer was that he had sent the only copy he had to the agent and it got lost in the mail. Even back then it was a lame story, and nowadays it's no excuse at all.)

For Safety's Sake, always keep a master copy of your work until the book itself is actually in print. If you are typing the beast by hand instead of using a computer, by all means make at least one photocopy (preferably two) since you don't have the added security of having it on a disk somewhere. Keep either your backup disks or an extra photocopy in a safety-deposit box, your best friend's basement or some other "off the premises" location, just in case of fire, flood or burglary. Although agents, publishers and the post office aren't known for losing things, sometimes that happens and you'll be far wiser and more secure knowing you have another copy available should something untoward happen.

 Asterisks are not commonly used in novels, as one doesn't usually have footnotes and such. However, in the flow of writing or even rewriting, you're bound to run across a fact, color or name that you want to verify for accuracy, but you don't want to take the time out to research it at the moment. I generally follow that word or sentence with an asterisk, simply to alert myself to go back and check this particular fact or spelling, date or location at a later time. As long as your editor understands that these asterisks are simply a form of shorthand for yourself, there's usually no problem with them, and you'll find them useful when you're preparing for the final editing, after the book is sold.

Blank Paper for Note-Taking during rewriting is essential for me. Depending on the size of the manuscript, this paper may be a handful of binder pages stashed at the end of the manuscript in the three-ring binder, or it may be a pad of yellow lined paper, which is easy to spot wherever I put it down. Either way, I keep it at hand as I do my final editing and *particularly* when rewriting.

Here I jot down everything I need to remember for future reference—the color of the heroine's eyes, which hand has the scar on it, what the name of the latest wolfhound is, whose birthday is when—and what page it lives on in the manuscript.

Then when I come to a later description of the heroine, the villain's hands, the favorite dog, etc., I can turn immediately to the note pages and confirm both what *and* where the earlier appearance was. For example: Has every reference to a hawthorn tree been when it was in bloom? Does the stage road always turn east at the base of the tree where the eagle lives, and if so, is that too repetitive? Again, this may sound petty, but readers notice things like this, and while even some of my favorite authors get repetitious, those are not their works that are among my favorites.

This is also a good time to write down the names of minor characters or locations—with the correct spellings. And if you delete a section in the rewriting, note it here (both chapter and page number you took it from, plus the name of the file you saved it in on the computer).

I note foreshadowing on these pages as well because I don't want to repeat the same phrases when the subject comes up again, and this way I can compare each mention and see how it builds in size and interest. This is also the place to write down exact quotes if you're going to use them again or if you want to avoid repeating that phrase, word for word.

Last Minute Changes get to be considered here. In a perfect world you wouldn't find major loopholes or new ideas at this stage of the game—you are, after all, almost finished with the writing part of your project.

But loopholes do surface and new ideas do intrude, sometimes well, sometimes miserably. Since this is your last chance to make major changes, correct whatever loopholes you can and note your *new* ideas on your pad. They could be as much a case of bridal nerves as brilliant inspiration, so sleep on them for a while before deciding whether to discard or incorporate them.

Final Version printouts take me several days and are quite taxing on my printer, so I tend to print whole sections as I go along, perhaps five or six chapters at a block, carefully stashing each in a binder set aside for the final product.

KNOWING WHEN IT'S FINISHED

Strange as that may sound, many artists have difficulty recognizing that they've done the best they can on a particular work, and they go on tinkering right into oblivion. Indeed, some novelists have a terrible time letting go of their work, their baby, their literary identity. One agent I know says she has to virtually steal fully realized manuscripts from one of her clients, who always wants to go on making just a few more corrections.

This can be a real trap. First, it keeps you from ever having to introduce your brainchild to the rest of the world. Most of us are a little leery about what kind of reaction our most recent efforts will bring forth, and if you're a first-time novelist, the anxiety can be high. But if you feel *too* shy and protective toward your literary offspring, it will never leave the nest.

Secondly, as an author you need to avoid the "carved in stone" attitude. This comes about when you've spent so much time making your work letter perfect, you aren't willing to consider ANY kind of change to it, including the suggestions of a professional editor. Writers who operate in this mode quickly get a reputation as being difficult and may sabotage their own careers this way.

Ideally, you want to find a balance between knowing you've made the work AS GOOD AS YOU CAN by yourself and being flexible enough to accept and consider an editor's suggestions. Admittedly, that's a delicate balance, but sooner or later you're going to have to show your book to other professionals, and one or more of them are going to suggest changes, the reasons for which will be explored in the next chapter.

Granted, it's a scary idea but a necessary step if you want to see your work published and have room to spread its own wings. In the end the rewards, in terms of attracting a good agent and solid sale, can be high points in your life, so surely it's worth a try!

PART THREE

When It's Done

CHAPTER TWELVE

Finding Pros
For Your Prose

F inding (and keeping) the right agent is often crucial to a writer's career. Few professional marriages are more important than that between author and agent, yet many authors—novice and master alike—go into the search for a new agent with more fear than foresight, trusting that blind luck will send them to the right representatives. Eager, scared, uncertain what to expect, one writer summed it up as "feeling like a mail-order bride . . . you just pray the professional who wants to handle you is someone you can put your faith and trust in."

Fortunately, most agents are both faithful and trustworthy. The vast majority are honest, caring professionals committed to selling manuscripts they believe in to publishers who don't have the time to read everything on the market and so rely on the agents' ability to send them things that are likely to fit their specific needs.

But if most agents are dedicated to their authors' welfare, why do so many authors complain that they can't find a good one? I personally think that's a reflection of how touchy the partnership is, rather than an indictment of agents as a whole.

Some agents and authors work well together in the beginning but are not temperamentally suited over the long haul, either because of personality quirks on both parts or the writer's ego getting out of hand. Sometimes the agent wants the author to write what the agent can sell rather than selling what the author is writing, which can be disconcerting. And sometimes an agent contracts with an author because the agent sees an easy sale—a flash in the pocketbook—and later the agent has no specific use for that writer and so simply ignores him.

If that happens, it's hard not to take it personally, instead of chalking it up to callousness on the part of the agent; after all, there are opportunists and quick-buck artists in every walk of life. Yet many a disgruntled author goes slamming out the door, embarking on a career of agency hopping, looking for the perfect agent and bad-mouthing everyone else.

That is not only unfair, it's also professionally stupid, and the best way to avoid it is to understand the limitations and parameters of your representative right from the start.

WHAT AN AGENT IS—AND ISN'T

I believe firmly that forewarned is forearmed, and the more you understand the agent's role, the less likely you'll be to cherish a lot of unrealistic expectations that leave you hurt, angry, disappointed or disillusioned.

One of the first expectations to get rid of is the notion that your agent is AUTOMATICALLY your friend. It's possible that, with time, the two of you will develop a deep friendship. But that doesn't happen overnight, and when you read chatty letters between author and agent, usually they are the result of *years* of working together. So keep your initial letters brief and professional, and don't take up the agents' time with notes about children, dogs or pet peeves. Let them make the first moves toward being personal friends if they want to—and if they have the time. Considering that something like thirty-five thousand new manuscripts get submitted to agents, editors and publishers every year, most publishing professionals are already fairly busy.

Keep in mind that your agent is a business cohort with whom there is a mutual dependency: Without her, you have little leverage with publishers; without you, she has no product to sell. An agent who smells a big sale will be on the phone to you frequently and eagerly, taking as much pride in closing a good deal for you as you take in having written the work to begin with. But when an agent no longer associates you with money and sales, your phone calls may go unanswered for weeks, your letters get lost and your submissions not read for months on end.

While there is no excuse for rudeness on the part of an agent, you need to remember that for this professional, time is literally money. Therefore agents are going to focus their time and attention on authors and books that are HOT and will get around to you (1) when they can or (2) when you provide them with an equally hot property.

Richard Curtis, who is himself an agent, has written a number of columns for and about writers, publishers and agents, most of which have appeared in the science fiction/fantasy magazine *Locus*. A compilation of these was published under the title *Beyond the Best Seller*, which provides a classic introduction to both the workings of the industry and the function of the agent. By all means look this one up, or get his *Mastering the Business of Writing*, which is specifically geared to the writer.

HOW IMPORTANT IS AN AGENT?

Sometimes people ask if they really need to have an agent. After all, 15 percent is a lot of money when you think about it. Can't the author just deal with the publisher directly? Sure she can, and come away with only three legs and no more warm woolly coat.

It's not that publishers are out to fleece the unwary, but they are in the business of making money off your product, and if they can do so without giving away any more rights than necessary, they'll try. Remember that ANY STANDARD CONTRACT DEVISED BY A PUBLISHER PROTECTS THE PUBLISHER, NOT THE AUTHOR.

Some publishing houses do accept unsolicited manuscripts. Designated as "over the transom" in the industry, they often languish in a huge "slush pile," collecting dust for months at a time. The first couple of pages will eventually be scanned by a weary reader who wades through innumerable novels every day and may, once every year or two, come up with one worth passing on for further scrutiny.

On the other hand, she may be suffering from dyspepsia, lack of sleep or thorough boredom when she reaches your tome and, after a cursory glance, toss it into the reject pile. Those legendary rags-to-riches stories you've read are just that—legends—because they occur so rarely.

Even if you find a publisher on your own who is making you an offer, I'd still recommend that you have an agent represent you simply because there are so many details you have no way of knowing about until long after you've signed them away. Since bringing your manuscript to the attention of a publisher is half of what an agent expects to do, it's usually not hard to get the agent's attention once you've already accomplished that.

SO WHAT DOES AN AGENT DO?

Agents come in all shapes and sizes, with a correspondingly wide— or narrow—range of interests. The most pretentious see themselves as literary maestros, arbitrators of taste and behind-the-scene shapers of literary careers and cultural history. The most casual simply like working with authors and want to see good books get published. The vast majority, of course, fall somewhere in between, hopefully combining the best qualities of both.

Basically an Agent is a Middleman

It's the agent's job to know the market: Who is looking for what; who got burned on which book and why; what is the hottest subject, the most popular cover style (yes, there are fads among jacket colors and designs); who is the newest talent, the most recent casualty. The agent keeps track of which publishing firms are about to go under, where his favorite editors have gone when changing jobs and who got the best deal for what.

Once an agent agrees to handle your manuscript, he'll make copies of it, send it out to the editors he thinks will be interested and sends you copies of the rejections if the first batch of publishers decline to make you immortal. If your agent has made multiple submissions of your manuscript, sending it to several publishers at once, there may be a small bidding war during which the price goes up, sometimes appreciably. Then your agent will counsel you as to which one to take and why.

If, on the other hand, your agent sets up an auction where everyone is invited to bid competitively for your work, you may have to take the highest bidder whether you want to or not, depending on the parameters the agent set up regarding marketing strategy and advertising budget, as well as your advance. Auctions are usually for major works that are expected to become bestsellers. They can be held for first novels just as for more established authors and are both very exciting and exhausting.

THREADING THE CONTRACT MAZE

Not only does an agent find someone willing to put up the money to publish your book, he negotiates your contract. Since every aspect of a contract is up for grabs until agreed to by both parties, it's hard to say that *all* contracts allow for this or that. However, a good agent will get you the most of everything he can, from a good advance to the best royalty schedule. Nor is that all. Beyond the basic publication of your book, a good agent will be looking for other places to sell your product.

Subsidiary Rights cover everything from book clubs to video/film rights, audiotapes, stage and radio presentations, as well as magazine excerpts and serialization. Each is considered a separate right, and in the give and take of negotiating with the publisher, your agent may have to give in on one point in order to get you a better deal on another.

Electronic Rights have become important because even though the delivering of books via computer hasn't been perfected yet, publishers foresee the day when books are downloaded rather than printed on paper, so naturally they want to keep control of what are called the "verbatim rights." This is the literal reproduction of your text electronically, and most agents recognize—and agree with—the publishers' determination to keep these rights to themselves; kicking up a fuss over them can be a deal-buster.

Another but slightly different aspect of electronic rights covers multimedia, graphics and games, and there can be lots of pushing and shoving between publisher and agent in this area. Some publishers are more flexible than others, but depending on how they plan to market your historical, they may just decide to hang tough.

Book Club sales are usually handled by the publisher, with you getting an agreed-on percentage of the sale. This is fairly standard procedure and needs to be left to the pros who are all familiar with each other.

British and Foreign Translations are subsidiary rights often used by an agent as bargaining chips to win concessions in other areas. She will protect as many of these rights as she can and at the same time get you the largest amount of advance money possible (unless you specify otherwise).

Advances are what most authors live on from day to day and can range from several thousand dollars for the completed manuscript of an unknown to a million dollars or more for an eight-page proposal by an author whose name has become a household word. Basically your advance is the publishers' prepayment of the royalties your book is expected to earn for you. For instance, if an author is going to get 10 percent of the cover price of a twenty dollar book, that royalty would be two dollars per book. If the publisher agrees to a twenty thousand dollar advance, it means the royalties earned on the first ten thousand books will be kept by the publisher to pay off the advance. Once the book has sold enough to pay back that advance against royalties, it's "earned out," and royalties on any future sales will go to the author.

Royalty Schedules are another part of the agent/publisher negotiation. The idea is pretty standard though the figures vary according to economic times, the cost of materials and printing and the agent's chutzpah. The schedule generally calls for an increase of royalties as the number of books sold increases. The usual range for hardcover books begins at ten percent for, say, the first ten thousand copies sold, increases to 12½ percent on the next ten thousand sales and caps out at 15 percent after twenty thousand books are sold. (Again, this is only an example; the rate of increase can vary from contract to contract and is often used as a bargaining chip by both sides.)

Mass-Market Paperbacks pay considerably less in royalties, with a spread of anywhere from 4 to 10 percent; if the rate is 7 percent on a seven dollar book, for instance, you'll see forty-nine cents per volume sold.

Trade Paperbacks are a kind of hybrid that from time to time look as though they'll become more popular than hardcover (which costs much more to produce) or mass-market paperbacks (which are cheaper but must sell many more copies). Trade paperbacks are the size of a hardcover, with equally good typeface and layout but without the board that makes traditional books' covers hard and therefore more durable in such circumstances as library use. (Unfortunately, with library budgets shrinking all over the country, that major market for hardcovers is shrinking.) Some agents consider a good trade paperback deal as strong as a good hardcover contract, but that may depend on your own agent's success or failure with these deals in the past.

Joint Accounting is a common practice when the publisher is buying several books, say, the one you've already written and the sequel the publisher wants to put out once your name is established. Basically joint accounting means that not only does the first book have to earn out before you see any royalties over and above your advance, any further money book one earns gets applied to paying back the *advance* you're given for book two. Consequently you don't see ANY additional funds for years, while the second book gets written and paid off. It is *not* an arrangement that is popular with most authors, and I've been told fewer publishers are insisting on it now.

And if keeping track of all this isn't enough, there's more besides. After your agent's made the sale and negotiated your contract, she should keep tabs on the production of your book, find out how big the print run is and when it will be released to the bookstores and be right there helping to talk it up when it comes out. In general you can say a good agent is your eyes and ears in the publishing world and acts as go-between for you and the publisher.

Sound complicated? You bet. But all of these are the necessities that go along with being published, and thank goodness agents want to handle them while you stay home and write!

Though some authors grumble at paying 15 percent to their agents, a good one is well worth that as she will save you time, guide your career, advise you on future projects and generally steer you through shark-infested waters. When you consider what all they have to know and juggle and how much energy they put into it if they are truly doing the job right, agents earn every penny of their commissions.

(For those who want to understand more thoroughly both their contracts and various other legal aspects of publishing, I suggest *Kirsch's Handbook of Publishing Law*, by Jonathan Kirsch. Kirsch is an author, a book reviewer and a practicing attorney specializing in the field. His book is not only lucid and useful, he breaks down the standard contract clause by clause, in terms the layman can readily understand. And he intersperses his explanations with anecdotes about specific cases. He also looks at idea protection, agent-author relationships, reversion of rights and copyright termination. As he takes pains to note, this is *not* a do-it-yourself book, but it does a great deal to explain many things, including when you do need to consult an attorney.)

NEVER GET BETWEEN YOUR AGENT AND THE PUBLISHER

After you've found your agent, step back and let her do her job. One British author who was picked up by a high-powered New York agent was so stunned at the amount of money the agent was asking for his manuscript, the author called the publisher directly and said he was sure there must be some mistake; of course he didn't expect the publisher to pay that much for his manuscript! Needless to say the agent was furious because after all her hard work in building up the importance of this international figure, her commission suddenly took a nosedive.

LOOKING FOR THE BEST

Basically anyone can hang out a shingle claiming to be a literary agent, regardless of his knowledge of publishing or the question of his ethics. And, unfortunately, a few shabby people have. Recently a very hungry author had to file court charges against his agent, who had taken the money from the publisher but never forwarded it to the client.

Fortunately THAT CASE IS A RARITY, and shocked the rest of the agents as much as it did the writing community. But it goes to illustrate the importance of knowing who your agent is. Most reputable agents nowadays belong to various professional groups ranging from the broader based Writers Guild of America (WGA) to the more specific Association of Authors' Representatives, Inc. (AAR). This latter group not only offers a brochure about agents and a list of their members for potential clients, but also publishes the standard of ethics that governs its members. To get a copy of both the roster and ethics, send a check for five dollars to AAR, 10 Astor Place, Third Floor, New York, NY 10003 along with a self-addressed stamped envelope with fifty-five cents in postage. It's a good investment that gives you a fundamental understanding to build on.

Lists of Agents are published by a number of people. The bibles of the industry, *Literary Market Place* (*LMP*) and *Writer's Market,* are huge compilations of who does what in publishing and how to reach them. Both publishers and agencies are listed, complete with blurbs about what they do or don't handle, who to contact, whether to query first and if they're willing to look at new authors. Since they are both extensive and expensive books that are frequently updated, you'll probably find them in the reference department of your public library. The annual *Guide to Literary Agents* (Writer's Digest Books) breaks down the information in a number of different ways: literary agents; script agents; fee charging or non-fee charging; agencies open to new clients, only published authors or only by referral.

Contracts Between Agents and Authors are pretty much an

individual thing. I know some powerful professionals who insist on them, and others of equal standing who figure that kind of agreement only works as long as both people make it work, and a piece of paper won't change that. It is assumed that you'll work only with one agent or agency, though sometimes personality problems or different market interests lead an author to change from one agent to another within the same agency. Certainly as a matter of personal ethics, you need to conclude your business with one agent before signing on with another. (Even if you change agents, the one who negotiated the contract continues to earn the commission from any money you make on that sale. The new agent is only entitled to money on what he sells new.)

Stealing Each Other's Clients is frowned on, and most agents adhere to an unspoken agreement about not luring authors away. But if they meet you at a conference, over lunch or through another writer, it's considered cricket for them to give you their cards, saying, "If you're ever inclined to look for a new agent, keep me in mind." By all means, keep those cards!

Never Pay Up Front to Be Represented. Occasionally I'll hear of someone getting a response to her manuscript that says, basically, "You've written a good book and if you pay me five hundred dollars, I'll represent you for a year." My reaction is to warn the author away from such things. A reputable agent accepts the up-front cost of finding you a publisher; she will benefit nicely *after* she's performed her services, and you should never expect to give her money beforehand.

Operations like this are more likely to be one of those fly-by-night "agents" who simply mails out your manuscript every so often without even conversing with the editor who's getting it. For goodness sake, you could do that yourself.

Reading Fees are something else again. In the past some agencies offered to read and critique an unknown author's manuscript for a set fee. Considering how many people want to get published and how much time it takes to read a manuscript, I can understand this practice. On the other hand, as one agent told me firmly, "Reading the submissions I've asked to see is one of the most important things I do." And the AAR, which originally allowed those agencies that had charged reading fees in the past to continue with the practice, has now specifically come out against it.

Agent Involvement is an amorphous area that's hard to generalize about. Some agents want to read every page of every submission *before* it goes to the publisher, even when it is in final edited form. Others are far more debonair, figuring that once they've sold the editor on the manuscript, the changes, improvements and rewrites are between the author and the editor. Be forewarned, however, that lack of desire to read the finished product may signal that your agent is not particularly interested in your work any longer, since the best agents I've known have been *very involved* with their authors' manuscripts. It is often this involvement with already contracted work that makes it hard for them to find time to read new authors' material.

Sometimes an agent will make a suggestion as to what you may change to improve the *salability* of the product. Generally when an agent that you feel comfortable with makes suggestions that relate to the marketability of the work, you should listen. He is on your side, after all. But if he starts making suggestions as to how to change story line, characters or dynamics, take the advice with a grain of salt; you are the storyteller here, and while the agent is basically saying, "what you've done isn't convincing enough," his solution may not be much better. My motto is I'll consider an agent's suggestion, but the only people I'm willing to totally change my manuscript for are the ones who are paying to produce it, that is, my publisher and editor.

GAUGING THE AGENT'S ATTITUDE

Generally an agent's reaction to your work is easy to read right from the start. It can range from lukewarm—maybe she knows someone who might, perhaps, be interested—to grand enthusiasm if she thinks she can make a quick or sizeable sale for you. But while they mostly represent the little guy as conscientiously as they do the big name author, you can't blame agents for putting the most immediate energy into the products that promise to bring in the biggest and quickest returns. So if you find they're too busy to take your call, answer your letter or get back to you about your manuscript, you're safe in figuring they don't see your work as best-seller material.

Unfortunately, best-sellers—even in the field of historical novels—don't come along every day. Most of us are mid-list authors, the cash cows that can be counted on to generate a little more than they cost to produce, and are treated accordingly.

HOW THE MONEY WORKS

It sometimes surprises people to discover that the money the publisher sends to the author goes directly to the agent. Depending on agency policy, the agent may deduct the cost of phone calls, copies, messengers and international postage, plus his commission, then send the remainder on to you. Some do not charge for phone calls, messengers and so forth, so AAR suggests you discuss this with any potential representative before making a commitment. In either case, having the money go through the agent is traditional and offsets the fact that there is no outlay required of you other than producing the manuscript.

As authors' legal representatives (some request Power of Attorney from their clients because of the many legal documents they handle), agents have certain financial and ethical obligations to their authors. While most are ethical in the handling of clients' funds, a few agents have been known to hold the authors' money some weeks longer than necessary, letting it accumulate interest in their own accounts while the authors keep checking empty mailboxes.

AAR has strong strictures against such behavior, and since different agencies have different policies as to how quickly they turn around the clients' funds, this is another area AAR urges authors and agents to talk over at the beginning so that each of you know what kind of time element to expect. Any contract that simply says your money will be sent on in a "timely manner" gives you little protection. And calling the publisher to ask where your statement and check are usually just gets you a secretary who says the check was approved weeks ago and sends you back to your agent again.

Just as you can't get a disinterested agent to call you back, you probably won't be able to track down any intentional wrongdoing: "The bookkeeper has been out sick." "The computer is new and we've lost time getting familiar with it." "It takes two weeks to get mail delivered from one building to another in New York City." You name it; a distracted, overworked or downright unethical agent can find an excuse that fits.

On the other hand, the publisher's secretary may be mistaken, or your editor may have authorized payment but your money is stuck in bookkeeping for weeks. One hardworking agent says she puts in more calls than she can count to the large, corporate publishers, trying to dislodge checks for her authors! So don't jump to the immediate conclusion that your agent is holding out on you, and do talk it over with her if the delay extends past your agreed-upon time.

Also remember that while you probably have only *one* book and *one* agent on which *all* your financial future hangs, the agent may be taking care of upward of twenty-five or thirty clients. While an agent needs to keep in touch and not leave her author sitting by the phone day after day waiting for the return call that was promised last week, by the same token you should pick up the receiver and call her a second time if she hasn't gotten back to you when she promised. Three calls a day are too many, and assuming the agent isn't representing you properly and deciding to call it quits without making a second effort may be precipitous on your part. All of this simply goes to show just how delicately balanced the agent-author relationship is.

While We're On Touchy Subjects, sometimes questions arise about who the agent owes his deepest allegiance to—you as the small author he's just taken on or the publisher with whom he's placed five or six expensive books a year over a long period of time. On the financial level it would be understandable if that agent was loathe to rock the boat on your behalf when trouble arises. However, GOOD AGENTS TAKE THEIR MORAL AND FINANCIAL DUTIES TO EVEN THEIR SMALLEST CLIENT SERIOUSLY. As my own agent points out, she finds that representing a big name with a publisher means she has more clout in protecting an unknown if there are any difficulties with the little guy's book.

If you come up against a problem with your publisher, write to your agent explaining your position, and ask him to look into it. If you're getting good representation, he will (1) immediately find out what's going on; (2) explain if you've misunderstood something; (3) inform you what can be done to correct the problem; and (4) actively defend you and your book if the publisher (or editor) is not living up to her end of the bargain.

If *none* of these things happen, chances are that agent has written you off, as you should him. There are sometimes extenuating circumstances such as personal problems or time conflicts within the agent's life, but this is your livelihood as much as his, and you deserve a professional who treats you like one in return. Give him one more chance to get back to you, and if you still don't hear, write a further letter suggesting that this partnership isn't working any longer. *Guide to Literary Agents* includes tips on how to gracefully end an author-agent relationship. It doesn't have to be slash-and-burn, and both you and the agent will feel better if it's handled without rancor.

Don't Give Up Hope. Whether you're a new author just starting to look for an agent or a seasoned professional back out there in limbo, keep in mind that there are many hardworking, reputable agents who will treat you with respect, understand the market you are writing for and give you excellent representation. You just need to spend some time finding the right one.

EAST COAST, WEST COAST

Many, but by no means all, major agents are located in New York City. There's a certain cachet about having a New York agent. She can go out to lunch with a different editor or publisher every couple of days, klatch about the price of paper rising so fast, listen to complaints about this or that author, critic or other publisher and generally be part of the loop. New York agents are in the know, have a personal touch and develop priceless contacts. Well, not quite priceless; that's what your 15 percent pays for.

Naturally, with the advent of e-mail, faxes, downloading and all the other electronic gadgetry that's followed on the wake of the telephone, an agent in California or Ohio has almost as easy access to the New York publishers as one based in Manhattan itself. Such far-flung agents usually go back to New York several times a year, meet with both potential authors and acquisition editors at writers and professional conferences, such as the ABA (American Booksellers Association), and sometimes attend the international book fair in Frankfurt as well. So it's no longer essential for your agent (or you) to live in or near New York City. And some authors go for years without ever laying eyes on their agents; a strong professional relationship doesn't require personal contact to be successful.

Agents Who Specialize in one kind of book or another—some do nothing but fiction or mysteries or are strongest in fantasy, YA (young adult) or nonfiction—can most easily be found through writers organizations already discussed. Unfortunately there aren't any such groups specifically for *historical fiction*, but both Western Writers of America and Romance Writers of America have chapters all over the country, and if your historical novel qualifies as either or both, you'll be able to get lists of reputable agents from other members.

Some agents prefer to stay flexible, reading all sorts of things because of their own eclectic interests and refusing to be pigeon-holed. Still, as in any human endeavor, after a bit agents will gravitate toward what their favorite editors are buying, so naturally they look for the kinds of manuscripts they know they can place. By the same token, when an editor gets a call from a particular agent, he is already predisposed to accept the work if that agent has sent him good things in the past.

Therefore you're better off looking for an agent who sells the *kind* of novel you write rather than one who tries to get you to write the kind of novel she can sell.

The best way to do that is to find out who represents the authors that write the same kind of book you do, or, as one agent asked me, "Whose audience are you trying to reach?" Frequently authors will thank their agents in a preface or acknowledgment, and armed with that name, you can try tracking it down in one of the literary directories. Or he may be mentioned in a magazine article in *Publishers Weekly* or *Writer's Digest*, both of which are well worth reading if you're serious about making this a career. Then too, the Internet is full of stuff about agents.

Writers Conferences and Workshops are another potential resource for information on agents. You don't have to be published to go to most local or state conferences, and many community colleges, extension courses, night-school classes and workshops are open to writers of every stripe. By all means attend these, as much for the people you'll meet and be able to network with as for the information shared in the actual classes or workshops.

Such conferences can pop up anywhere. There is one held every March in Fresno, California, an agricultural town that is not exactly known for it's cultural milieu. Put on by Writer's International Network-Writer's Inter-age Network (WIN-WIN), the three-day event is called "The How To Get and Stay Published Conference." Over the years the organizers have gotten some of the best nationally known authors, publishers, agents, editors and screenwriters to come as speakers. The result is a chance to meet professionals you would otherwise never get to see in person, as well as an opportunity to learn about the current marketplace and possibly find the perfect agent for your stuff.

LARGE AGENCY OR SMALL

If you're a first time novelist, look for agencies that encourage new authors; they will say so in their blurbs in most guides. Some agents are tremendously excited about finding new authors with salable material. Which of the book clubs will want them? How will the critics respond? Can this writer's work develop "legs," becoming so popular it all but runs out the doors of the bookstores, and is there any chance of film or TV deals? So don't assume that just because you're an unknown you won't get a good agent's full attention. For many the excitement of the discovery is half the reason they stay in the business.

There are pros and cons about going with a large agency as compared to a smaller one. In a large agency you have more chance of being handed off to someone who really knows and enjoys your field. Large agencies usually have their own sub-rights specialists (guarding and/or selling your subsidiary rights) and often have connections with agents in other countries. (International sales are generally much smaller than U.S. sales simply because the populations are smaller, but they can add not only prestige but a little extra money to your coffers.) The biggest problem with going to a big agency is that you'll probably be only one of a large number of hopeful beginners and may find yourself treated like part of the cattle call.

Smaller agencies have fewer clients and may be more limited in how much of the publishing field they can play but may well give you more personal service. Just because they're small doesn't mean they don't pack a solid wallop, so you can judge best by who they represent rather than how many. Some agents will give you a list of clients if you ask, though that policy varies from agency to agency.

It's worth putting real time and energy into finding the right representative, as your agent can make or break your career. An agent doesn't have time to be interviewed *before* she shows an interest in your work, but once she wants to represent you, there will probably be a long phone call during which you'll each be taking the measure of the other and deciding how comfortable you'll be in a professional partnership. By all means make up a checklist of things to ask, such as those recommended by AAR, and be sure to cover the same information with each agent so you'll have a basis for comparison. *Guide to Literary Agents* also has an example of an evaluation page, which includes more subjective things such as

"Asked *me* lots of questions" and "Offered references without asking." That, however, comes down the line, after you've gotten the agent to read your manuscript.

QUERY LETTERS

Once you've developed a list of agents you want to contact, it's time to make up a query letter.

This is a ONE-PAGE, carefully crafted letter stating what you've written and inquiring whether the agent would like to see it. It may take you several days to write it, and even then you may want to let it be for a while, then go back and reread it; it's that important.

The best queries follow a simple formula that was taught to me by an editor's assistant who knew exactly what his boss was looking for.

Paragraph One is short: I have a completed manuscript of _____ pages, entitled _____ , which is about (one sentence summation) _____.

Paragraph Two is the bulk of the letter, and explains what the book is *without* trying to tell the story itself. You want to whet the reader's appetite to see the manuscript, not condense it for him.

This is also the place to mention what makes this book unique, and if there are any names to be dropped, this is where to say "So-and-so has encouraged me in this project," or "_____ of Such and Such publishers has expressed interest in seeing the completed work."

You don't need to go into your own credentials; the agent's interest is not in you, but in your manuscript, so make it the center of all attention.

Paragraph Three is another shorty: If you would be interested in seeing any or all of my manuscript, please let me know.

Sincerely,

In my query letter about the Guinevere books, paragraph one stated that this was a psychological portrait of the members of King Arthur's Round Table as seen through the eyes of his queen, Guinevere.

Paragraph two pointed out that these were the archetypical characters of western civilization, and that I was dealing with them in a realistic and historically accurate fashion. I also was able to mention several successful authors who had, indeed, encouraged my work. (Though neither agreed to read it then or later, both had said they thought it was a fine idea. NEVER say you've got an endorsement you don't have. One major company recently paid a great deal for a young man's submission because a famous author had praised it lavishly. When the author announced that he didn't know the young man and had never seen the manuscript, the legal fur flew all over New York. That's the kind of thing that can cost publishers big money and get you blackballed permanently.)

The central paragraph of your query, and your single sentence summation of your work, are the most important aspects of your letter. There is a real knack to writing queries, just as there is for writing proposals, and I suggest you look into the books on the subjects.

Once you've gotten your query letter in hand, send it out to four or five of the top agents on your list. It's quite reasonable to send several at once, though you should mention that you are querying others, and be prepared to make and send as many copies as necessary, if they all answer in the affirmative. (An agent may request an exclusive look at your work for three to four weeks. If the response was quick and pleasant, by all means give her that courtesy. It also assures that you won't be waiting around for months until she finally gets around to you. If you're *not* thrilled with her response, however, then you need to decide if you want to comply with the exclusivity request. You don't have to, after all, if there are others who are also eager to read your manuscript.)

THE WAITING GAME

You should get a response from a query letter within a week or two since it can be answered by postcard. Some may take a little longer, and a few may not answer at all (bad manners abound in every industry, and you wouldn't want to be represented by people that lazy). Some may decline gracefully, and others ask for anything from the first thirty pages (plus synopsis) to the whole manuscript.

Send Only and Absolutely What They Request

This is crucial. There are few things more aggravating than requesting to see the first thirty pages of a work only to be inundated by two hundred! It shows the author doesn't take instructions well or is intent on stuffing the whole thing down everyone's throat. Believe me, if agents want to see the whole manuscript, they'll ask for it; they are never shy.

Also, never send several versions of the same thing. This is extremely unprofessional; it shows that you haven't been willing to bite the bullet and make your own choices, and *if* the agent bothers to read multiple versions, he's likely to become too bored with it to do it justice.

If you're having trouble deciding between one version and another, kick it around with another writing friend, not a professional, unless the professional has asked to look at several versions.

This sharing with other authors, along with networking to keep abreast of what is happening in the industry, is one of the best reasons I know to take part in writers conferences, workshops and local groups. It helps tremendously to have others to bounce ideas off of, to ask for their reactions to this version or that, to discuss how best you—or they—can bring out what nuances, etc.

Always Send A Copy or second printout in answer to an agent's request, and keep an exact duplicate for yourself. With photocopying having replaced carbon paper and both floppy diskettes and hard drives storing your magnum opus somewhere in a computer, there's absolutely no excuse for you to lose your manuscript. But once it's sent, don't make changes or you'll get confused over who has what version!

Overnight Or Priority Mail is worth the price, both because you'll have proof of delivery (sometimes things do get lost) and because you want to strike while the agent's interest is hot. And you should include postage and a mailing label, or a self-addressed stamped packet in which the agent can return the work when finished with it.

Don't Call Me, I'll Call You is the standard response of agents, producers and such in the theater, and the same holds true in publishing. NEVER BUG AN AGENT. Most of them need two to three months to get to a new manuscript, even if it's one they've requested. (Six weeks used to be the accepted time, but as one professional suggests, the advent of word processing has turned everyone into authors churning out manuscripts at a horrific rate!) Anyhow, give the agent the time specified in *LMP* and remember that we've all gone through it.

Some agents will drop you a card saying they've gotten your

manuscript, but most won't. You can include self-addressed stamped postcards and ask them to let you know they received the packages intact.

If You Haven't Gotten Any Response By The Time They Themselves Requested, By All Means Call; you aren't bugging them if you play according to their rules, and something untoward might have happened to your book. If the agent hasn't bothered to read it by then, go ahead and ask that it be sent back. Or, if she still professes great interest, leave it with her on a nonexclusive basis. Again, this is one of those things to play by ear, and take into account who else is clamoring for it, or how few other replies you've had.

If all this sounds uncomfortably cold and businesslike, remember that you wrote your book for the love of it, but agents sell books to make a living. It won't hurt their feelings to have you take it back, and every day they put off reading your work, they risk having some other agent sweep you up enthusiastically.

CHAPTER THIRTEEN

The Next Step

O nce you've found your agent and your manuscript is launched upon the literary seas, you've a right to feel like Columbus about to sail off the edge of the earth; with any luck, you'll be bumping into the world of editors, publishers and galley slaves—the latter being yourself. It may be exciting, frustrating, heartbreaking or thrilling, depending on a number of factors you can't control. But the one thing you're likely to discover is that it isn't at all what you expected.

PUBLISHING—A CHANGED WORLD

It's easy to conjure up pictures of publishing as it used to be—the old-time gentlemen's profession, where agents are your friends and both editors and publishers believe so strongly in your talent, they'll stand by you even if you produce something that doesn't sell well initially.

There was a time when that was the case, when adventurous agents, exceptional editors or individual publishers developed stables of talented new wordsmiths, guiding, coaching and supporting them until the public began to pay them their due.

But those times are long gone. Some time after World War II smaller independent publishing houses began to be gobbled up by larger ones, and eventually the larger ones were subsumed by bigger conglomerates that are run by controllers, treasurers and bottom-line people who could care less whether the product is quality books or truck tires, as long as the right number of units gets sold and the bottom line looks good.

It's sort of like little fishes inside of bigger fishes, most all of which are inside of a few giant fishes, whose financial welfare dictates what happens to everyone else. Thus you have a publishing house with a great number of "imprints" under its umbrella. Some were formed specifically to be under the parent organization, while others had been major houses in their own right in the past.

The different imprints use the distribution, advertising and administrative departments of the parent company, with the various publishers having different degrees of autonomy and agents treating them as more or less separate houses.

Publishing can be a chancy occupation. One hears of an editor going out to lunch and coming back to find his imprint doesn't exist any more, the entire house having been expunged, and everyone suddenly unemployed. Worse yet, from a writer's point of view, the books in progress under that imprint become orphans with no one to guide them through the intricacies of getting printed. While orphan books are not an everyday occurrence, the concept is important enough to talk about a little later.

PUBLISHERS HAVE CHANGED, TOO

Book publishing has been a commercial venture ever since William Caxton printed the first book in English, back in 1475. Yet for the most part publishers cared as much about their books—and the content thereof—as they did about their profits. Unfortunately, with the takeover by megacorporations publishers have been forced to focus more on the business aspect of the profession and less upon the literary. As one young woman in charge of her own imprint told me, she simply didn't have time to read every book she published; as long as the book sold and her imprint showed a profit, the corporate bosses would be happy.

Even those who care deeply about their books and authors are constantly pressured by the marketing and accounting executives—the "bean counters" as one editor called them. It's the bean counters who decide what books will most likely sell and what not, which translates to you as yes or no about buying your manuscript.

There are many fine people in publishing, but as in all the glamor industries that are governed by huge corporations (records, films and books), there are many who are in it for the power and glitz. These people see the musician, filmmaker or author simply as a producer of merchandise to be hyped, and the moment the trend turns elsewhere, so does their interest, even if they've already bought your manuscript.

If that happens, it doesn't mean your book is bad or your writing lacks talent. In today's publishing world talent has little to do with anything. In fact, don't be surprised if you get rejection letters saying, "Good characterizations, well written, finely crafted story, but . . ." Basically that says the reader of your work recognized its quality, but because everyone's looking for last year's megaseller in this year's jacket, the publisher hesitates to invest in something new. So if you keep getting praise for your writing but no sales, it probably means either the publisher's afraid to take the chance or the bean counters have said there's no money to risk on an unknown's work, no matter how good it is.

And money is the deciding factor here. As the price of paper increases (from 50 to 100 percent in 1995 alone, depending on the company), the cost of publishing a book goes up. That's even more frightening when you consider that reading has become a luxury, a recreation that has to compete not only with softball or sports on the tube, but also with movies, walking, talking, shopping and surfing the Internet. Books now are bought out of discretionary funds, and new authors are seen as unproven commodities, which makes them all the more risky.

Then, too, books weigh a lot and are expensive to ship. It used to be that a bookstore could order four or five copies of a novel, and if it had two left after a specified length of time and needed the shelf space, the store could return the books at no charge. Since the early 1990s, however, it's the little guy who has to pay the return postage. Consequently most stores order only one or two copies of a new author's book; if they sell both copies there's a sigh of relief, but no one wants to take a chance on ordering more, unless the thing turns into another *Bridges of Madison County* (more on that in chapter fourteen).

When you understand both how publishing has changed and the amount of money it costs to edit, print, market and distribute a book, you can see why corporate publishers are cautious about purchasing anything. And as one insider pointed out, this caution leads to spending megabucks on the sure thing and giving little or no support to new, unknown authors. Which is, of course, why you need an enthusiastic agent.

WHICH MANUSCRIPTS SELL

Sometimes a publisher agrees with an editor that a particular book ought to be published just because it's a good work well written, but usually there's a market force driving the decision.

These forces take many shapes. Perhaps some other publisher made a best-seller out of a book like yours, and everyone who hasn't got a similar work wants one. (Just look at all the books about angels that flooded the bookstores in the early 1990s!) Or, as with Parke Godwin's *Sherwood*, the publisher wants something to tie to a big-name movie that's coming out several years down the road. Or the publisher wants to take advantage of a national anniversary coming up—did you really think it was a coincidence that *Centennial* came out in time for the 1976 celebrations?

These market forces are not new, of course. In 1935 Harold Latham, vice-president and editor in chief of Macmillan Company, was frantically looking for a novel set in the South because Erskin Caldwell's *Tobacco Road*, a gritty, realistic work about rural southerners, had sold remarkably well for another publisher. Macmillan Company wanted to exploit reader interest in the region, but Latham needed a book already written because there wasn't time to wait while one of his already contracted authors wrote one. So when he left for Atlanta he wasn't looking for an American classic set during the Civil War, but simply a manuscript that would give his company a share of the market.

At first Margaret Mitchell, who was squiring him around the city meeting all sorts of other people, denied having written a novel; when she finally allowed she had a manuscript, she said it wasn't ready to be read. Eventually she went home and collected all the bits and pieces that she'd stored under the bed, behind the sofa, and every other place she'd stashed them over the years. On the train ride north Latham waded into the stack of bags, boxes and envelopes full of half-scenes, whole chapters, occasional repeats and some big gaps, all out of order, but oh, so readable! He stayed up most of the night reading, and the rest is publishing history.

That was a case where the vice-president of the publishing house was involved. Usually, unless your agent is convinced she can sell your work as a best-seller, your manuscript will simply be read by an editor, and here is where you're most likely to find your book's best friend.

EDITORS—WHAT THEY ARE AND DO

Some authors will tell you that good editors are in short supply, while others have found marvelously helpful editors for whom they thank their lucky stars each night. But whether you love your editors or hate them, it's worth understanding both their function and the obstacles they face.

Normally your agent will have submitted your manuscript to one or more editors who have evinced interest when the subject was brought up either over lunch or on the phone. In a large house this might be an acquisitions editor—someone who specializes in deciding what to recommend the publisher buy.

With a more moderate sized publisher, the same editor that reads your manuscript will also be editing it, once he convinces his superiors it is a viable product, worth investing thousands of dollars in. This means that the editor has stood up for your work right from the beginning. Occasionally an editor will simply be assigned a particular manuscript or author, which need not be bad but often this editor doesn't have the same initial enthusiasm that's found when editors choose their books themselves.

Either way, once you've signed the contract and the manuscript has been turned over to the publisher, you'll be dealing with the editor, who is the link between the publisher and the author. In most cases you'll never meet the publisher or talk over editing problems with them, though you may talk with the editor for several hours every week during the most difficult times.

There seem to be more women editors than men, and as they're usually overworked and underpaid, there's a fair turnover in the profession. Additionally, it's a stressful occupation, and the burnout rate is high. One young woman who truly loved working with books and authors classified hers as "the most wonderful and exhausting job in the world!"

(Whether the person who edits your work is male or female, don't take umbrage if his or her title is editorial assistant; any editor who's too busy to edit your work wouldn't give it the kind of attention it deserves anyway, and an editorial assistant will. Believe me, assistants can be worth their weight in gold, so treat them with the same respect you'd give their bosses. Someday they may be taking their boss's place, after all.)

Usually an editor will either meet with you or have an extensive phone conference right at the beginning, possibly even before convincing the publisher to buy your work. This is the time to really feel each other out; the editor will be trying to determine how reliable or difficult you'll be, and you should be finding out how the editor sees your book—for example, what, if any, plot, focus or sequence changes he thinks should be considered.

WITH LUCK YOUR EDITOR WILL COME TO KNOW AND LOVE YOUR BOOK AS MUCH AS YOU DO and you'll get to know each other pretty well as she (or one of her cohorts) takes you step-by-step through the process of getting your book published.

CONTENT EDITING

After the contract is signed, your editor will read the manuscript through a second time, looking for places where the pace lags, the material is repetitive or contradictory, there are gaps or loops in the narrative thread or your logic goes bonkers. This is a general reading for content, structure and places that can be improved.

Listen To Your Editor

A good editor comes to the work wanting to see the book's potential realized and will have a less biased eye than you can ever have. If he says a chapter is extraneous, don't freak out over the splendid writing you're giving up; take the salient points you needed to make in that chapter and figure out how you can slide them in elsewhere.

Good editors are not always looking for things to excise. A caring editor will suggest that you add scenes and go into further detail on things that you may have glossed over—*if* that will make the work stronger in his eyes.

Sometimes an editor gets caught between wanting to encourage you to flesh out some scene or character and having to tell you that the publisher is demanding you cut out fifty, sixty, maybe even seventy pages in order to keep the cost of manufacturing down. (If you're a new author, the publisher will want to keep your book priced low enough to appeal to the casual browser, and cutting down the number of pages is the best way to cut down on the overall price.)

It will probably take your editor several months—maybe more— to get the first edited version back to you. (You should establish some sort of time line when you first get to talking seriously.) Take this time to go through your original manuscript and check out every asterisk you sprinkled through the text, whether it's a question of spelling an archaic city's name right, finding the perfect flower for the time and place or calculating how long it would take a royal progress to move from one camp to another. These are all the last little research things that won't change the story but may mean rewriting a sentence here or there.

Naturally as you track down each asterisk, you can get rid of it, which will give you a cleaner manuscript to work on when your editor sends you back his content suggestions. Probably you'll have a month or two to make major changes as editors know you can't just pull them out of the thin air. And he's likely to expect to talk with you occasionally during that time.

Some authors get very prickly about making changes, as though their prose were deathless and any suggestion by an editor was a personal affront. Some even argue over cutting individual words, which is not only a waste of time but a good way to get a reputation for being a prima donna! Remember, no one sentence is so price-less it can't be cut; if you're unable to put the good of the whole book before the cleverness of a phrase, you should stick to writing epigrams.

That is not to say that editors don't make mistakes, ask for the impossible or misunderstand where you want to go with something. It just means that you need to discuss whatever reservations or balkiness you feel with that editor so the two of you can agree as to what should be done.

Yes, There Are Difficult Editors

For all that I've had good relations with mine, I've certainly seen and heard some of the battles that can come about when editor and author don't get along. Sometimes it happens because of basic personality conflicts, with each disliking or distrusting the other's attitude, work habits or concept for the book. Sometimes it's because the editor is overworked and burned out, didn't want your book to begin with or, as some writers claim, is a frustrated author who uses her blue pencil to attack those who can write when she can't. (As a blanket indictment this is unfair, for I've found that thwarted authors often make the most compassionate and caring editors!) At any rate, if you have occasional difficulty with your editor, remember she's human too, with bad days, rotten colds, tremendous pressures from her work schedule and (usually) pretty low pay.

Still, if disagreements become chronic and tempers fray, the overall book will be affected, to say nothing of your peace of mind.

So if it becomes a pattern, go ahead and call your agent about it. He may have some insight that will help or may be able to talk with the editor or publisher discreetly. If, however, you have trouble with one editor after another, you'd do well to reassess your own attitude.

One of my editors told me that she pushes for important changes three times; if the author can't come up with a better solution after trying three alternatives, she lets it be. It's certainly to your best interest to work with your editor, not against her, but she needs to understand there may be some things you simply can't rework satisfactorily.

When you've addressed the various content or sequence changes your editor has suggested, you send the edited version back to her. At this point I make a totally new printout, but you and your editor can best decide if that's necessary.

FINE-TUNING

Line Editing is the next step. In some publishing houses the line editing is also done by the style editor, while in others it's the content editor who goes over the whole manuscript yet again. In any event, this editor looks for all the little things that will improve clarity or pace. Generally there will be a *long* list of notes with the page and line number called out for each sentence, word or idea you need to tighten up. I've seen these notes run to ten or fifteen single-spaced typed pages for a whole manuscript, but also noticed that while some sections had four or five different line items per page, others didn't have any comments for most of a whole chapter. When I asked my editor about this, she laughed and said there's obviously some days when she felt pickier than others. She also went on to say that if editors can't find something to improve, they feel they're not doing their job properly.

On the line-edited copy you need to address every one of the editor's concerns, writing out what you did or didn't do in response if you aren't in agreement with her or checking it off if you concur with her suggestion. Again, if you find something particularly bothersome or confusing, most editors encourage you to call and discuss it. At that point you and she can establish if you need to print out corrected pages or the whole chapter if the pages are so messy they demand reprinting.

(If you can't make a new printout of the corrected pages, retype them and send a photocopy so that everyone is working with the same material. And always date your pages.)

The Copy Editor now takes over your pruned and polished manuscript. He puts in (or takes out) commas, semicolons, ellipses, apostrophes and anything else necessary to bring the final product up to the publisher's standard style. There are many good (and friendly) copy editors, and they should all be treated as gifts from God, for they come to your work fresh and often catch little things that you and your primary editor have lived with so long, you no longer notice. So be nice to him, even if his punctuation drives you crazy.

On my first book I asked my agent just how much I had to accept the blue-pencilled copy editing, and he gave me a classic answer: "It's your name, not hers, that will go on the cover of the book . . . so it should be the way *you* want it in the final version." That doesn't give you carte blanche to challenge everything editors suggest—they may well have a better eye than you or better grasp of punctuation—but if the editing actually changes what you want to accomplish, stick by your guns.

Funny little things show up in copy editing, such as the fact most Easterners use a lot more *thats* than Westerners do, for example, an Easterner would say, "such as the fact *that* most Easterners." This one is so common, it seems to be a regional pattern rather than a personal quirk, but I've also run into copy editors who hated contractions, or compound sentences, or sometimes noted with exasperation that I used far too many parallelisms (something I still do not understand the definition of, much less how to correct).

Anyhow, the best thing to do is to reach some compromise; I usually concede anything that doesn't change the cadence of a sentence but delete every extra *that* and fight to keep contractions because they're so much more in keeping with how people actually speak. (Interestingly, many authors mention that if an editor wants to change one word in a sentence, they may agree but generally rewrite the entire sentence in order to keep the right rhythm and fall. It's a sort of "change one, change 'em all" response because most writers *hear* the words as they compose, and while they aren't necessarily set in stone about specific words, they want to retain the voice.

Remember that in the long run, NO EDITOR HAS A RIGHT TO SET YOUR WORK IN TYPE IN ANY FORM YOU HAVEN'T

APPROVED. Occasionally one hears horror stories of whole sections being edited or rewritten without the author's permission. That is, fortunately, very, very rare and probably is grounds for suit, though if the changes were made before you approved the galleys, then you weren't on your toes when reading those beasties.

Galleys are the next step, and correcting them can indeed feel like slave labor. In actual fact, galleys are long, continuous strips of paper on which your priceless words are set in type. They are the first tangible proof this monster is going to see the light of day, possibly the most exciting thing you've ever seen and usually just as daunting. Because it is now set in final type form, you have to go over *every* word looking for typos or misspellings, lines left out— or repeated—mistakes on your part (surely his eyes weren't two different colors in chapter four?) or the person who translated it to the printed page (just what is the word *qwinzelwithy* supposed to mean?).

Not only do you have to read these pages slowly and carefully— sometimes even checking against your copy of the line-edited manuscript—you usually have only ten days to two weeks to turn them around because by the time these pages are set in type, everyone is scrunching schedules like mad! It seems to be industry-wide, and all any author has to do to elicit immediate sympathy and understanding from all others is to say, "I'm working on galleys."

You are not the only one checking for typos; often galleys are sent not only to an outside proofreader who's never seen the material before, but also to your line editor, the philosophy seeming to be that the more eyes that check the galleys, the better.

This is your last chance to make changes. (The publisher will charge you if there are very many, and if you actually rewrite a sentence or two, try to match the same number of characters or at least lines so the typesetters don't have to change page breaks throughout the rest of the chapter. If you don't do that, the publisher will assess a charge for every page.

In any event, working on galleys means you want to be mentally fresh in order to focus on each and every comma, with your yellow pad at hand for any last minute notes.

BEHIND-THE-SCENES TIGER

Remember that editor who convinced the publisher to buy your manuscript, then went over it page by page not just once but three or sometimes four times and spent hours on the phone with you ironing out various wrinkles? Well, while you went on with style editing and typesetters, she was fighting like mad to get you some kind of decent cover, reasonable jacket copy, quotes from other authors and a solid place in the season's line.

These are the behind-the-scene activities people rarely think of that can make the difference between a good solid book release and one that gets lost in the shuffle. It is also here that you'll discover just what your publisher is going to do with your work.

Most contracts specify that a publisher has up to eighteen months to prepare the manuscript for publication. In actual fact, turnaround from completed manuscript to "pub date" (the official date listed for your book's publication) can be anything from six months on, and if publishers are incredibly excited they can bring out hardcover books in much shorter time—just look at the O.J. Simpson library that emerged even as the trial went on. But the average time frame is somewhere between six months and a year, with a year and a half being on the far end of things.

During this time the rest of the books that will comprise the list of titles for that season's "line" will be in the works as well, vying for advertising money, art department interest and sales force attention. So part of your editor's job is to be in there making sure your work gets its fair share of the pie.

Spring Line and Fall Line are holdovers from the days when shipping was controlled by the weather. Even though modern technology no longer makes delivery in the winter months a problem, publishers still adhere to the tradition of a spring line and fall line. Big fluffy works come out in the spring—just in time to take to the beach—while the heavy hitters and name authors make up the fall line, in time for Christmas shoppers.

New authors are often introduced in the spring so as not to have to compete for review space and consumer dollars with the megastars in the autumn. This can be a definite advantage, as even a splendid work by a lesser known author can be overlooked if everyone is busy reviewing the latest Stephen King.

Depending on your publishing house and the position of your editor in that house (it can be *very* hierarchical, and a new author frequently goes to the least powerful editor), he may have some say in when your work hits the stores. Certainly he will try to get it into the most appropriate market slot for the sales force, which isn't always easy, as you'll see when we get to marketing.

By now it should be clear that your editor is crucial to the successful launching of your book, and if you lose your editor somewhere along the line, your book can become an orphan.

Orphan Books don't happen all that often but should be avoided whenever possible. Since your editor midwifes your creation, wrapping it in swaddling clothes and presenting it to the publisher, art department, promotional people, reviewers, awards committees, to say nothing of the sales force at the usual sales meetings, losing him means there's no one to stand up for your work. Whether he leaves because he's changing jobs, moving away or taking time off for health reasons, there's no one to argue your work should be listed as fiction, not romance; that it deserves a real cover, not a pinup fantasy; that there are numerous historically oriented publications that should know and review your work, etc.

Orphan books usually end up any old place it's convenient to stash them. Chances are your publisher will be too busy to take over the care and feeding of it, and other editors are looking after their own little darlings and won't have much time or enthusiasm for one that's been abandoned.

There's not much you can do about it, but it helps to establish what the editor's personal plans are *before you sign your contract.* If she says things like, "I'll be following my husband to Europe as soon as I've finished content editing your work," *take heed.* Remember, her job is far more than word arrangement and text improvement, and without her guidance your book is a helpless babe in the woods. You may still choose to go with that publishing firm; just recognize that your work may be handicapped before it even gets into print.

TITLES AND ARTWORK

When I do public speaking engagements about writing, I'm always bemused at how much power the audience thinks authors have. Usually they are very surprised to learn that we have only limited input on the titles of our books and little or no say over the cover. Sometimes the contract will say something to the effect that title and cover art are "subject to the approval of the author," but if you think that means you can stop a disaster from happening, you're as naive as I was in the beginning.

Titles are particularly important. The more ornate and flowery, the more likely you are to see your historical classified as a romance and given a Harlequin type cover. (There is nothing wrong with this if that's what you want, but if you haven't written a women's romance, the chances are the romance reviewers will hate it, claiming, for example, it isn't juicy enough.)

Most of us need a working title and will have a title on the finished manuscript, which may or may not influence the publisher. Try to pick one that is simple and direct, that doesn't equivocate and does say what the subject is about. For instance, originally I'd wanted to see my Guinevere books come out as *Guinevere I, II* and *III*—no question there what the subject was, or the sequence. Alternatively, I suggested *Arthur's Bride, Britain's Queen* and something having to do with legends and lovers for the third one. Short and to the point, they seemed to me to at least get the idea across. Unfortunately I'd been using a quote from a poem for the working title, and no one would consider the other options. So my Guinevere ended up with very flowery titles and froufrou covers. Only the third volume, *Guinevere: the Legend in Autumn*, has her name in it, mainly because my new editor fought so hard for it.

It is a lesson worth learning. Michener's *Hawaii, Chesapeake* and *Alaska* all stake out their territory. Even *The Source* and *Caravans* carry the sense of their areas (Palestine and Afghanistan, respectively). And you better believe I'll go to the wall over *Sierra* when the time to settle on a title comes around.

Everyone has problems with titles. Margaret Mitchell scribbled *The Road to Tara* (and Scarlett was named Pansy) in the manuscript form of *Gone With the Wind.* No one really liked either name, but *Tomorrow Will Be Fair* and *Another Day* weren't much better. At the very last minute Mitchell happened on a poem that included the words "gone with the wind" and suggested it to Latham, who approved immediately. Interestingly, she had used the phrase midway through the book, when Scarlett, faced with the devastation of Twelve Oaks and the other grand plantations all around her, wonders, "was Tara also gone with the wind which had swept through Georgia?" but no one had caught its potential. Scarlett herself got christened about the same time—just before going to press—when Mitchell picked the name from the manuscript where it was noted that the Scarletts were ancestors of the O'Haras.

In the end it was Mitchell who suggested both title and character name, but you should never discount a good suggestion just because it isn't your own. It's *that* important. And more than one strong title has come from brainstorming between author, editor and even friends.

Covers are another area entirely. Your publisher may or may not kick some ideas around with you, but even if you both agree verbally on something, the translation into a painting can be very different from what you thought you agreed to.

Your editor will have some limited input and can try to get you a cover that's appropriate to the subject or mood of your opus, but most cover decisions are based on marketing agendas and the current trends in cover art. Occasionally really good ones show up: Parke Godwin's *Robin Hood* covers, both in hardbound and paperback, are excellent; they read well from across the room, indicate the time and conflict and are thoroughly masculine in concept—no likelihood they'll be mistaken for Harlequins.

But not infrequently authors are unhappy with their covers. Part of the problem has to do with the fact that the artists commissioned to paint book covers are not expected to read or adhere to the books' contents. Usually they are told what to paint by the publisher and art director (who haven't read the book either, but know what market they want to appeal to—war, adventure, fantasy, women's romance, etc.).

By the time you see it, the artwork is a fait accompli, and neither you nor your editor can do anything about the fact that your protagonist's favorite black horse has been turned into an Appaloosa, the famous wall at Gettysburg now surrounds a replica of Independence Hall from Philadelphia and a Renaissance church rises out of the mists in Dark Ages Britain. Often the results are ludicrous, if infuriating.

Does anyone besides the author care? Well, yes and no, but there's virtually nothing you can do except mutter, "How nice," when you really want to scream, "But it has nothing to do with the book I wrote!"

Unfortunately screaming won't do anything but get you a bad reputation, because if you do make enough fuss to be heard in New York, you'll come up against the very reasonable argument that the publisher put up all that money to get your book into print and is jolly well going to market it in the way the company thinks will best recoup its investment. Forget that the cover is so murky and undefined it looks like an algae pond from four feet away. Forget that the lettering is so thin, no one can read it from across the aisle (another advantage of brief titles: fewer letters and bigger type, yet more artwork shows). And last of all, forget that your homely tomboy is now a raven-haired temptress full of pride and arrogance. The publisher knows what sells, and you should stick to writing books and not fuss about covers, even if you've had years of experience in advertising before you became a novelist!

Besides, if you make too many waves, you run the risk of being classified as a difficult author, which is definitely not what you want.

IT'S A SMALL WORLD

Big time publishing in New York is much smaller than most people realize. Everyone knows everyone else, goes to the same parties, fights for the same reading public, wines and dines the same big-wigs and follows the careers of the same authors.

Consequently, if your agent, editor and publisher are all excited about your book, everyone in the industry will hear about it and be eager to see for themselves. By the same token, if you get a reputation for being difficult, unreliable, hard to work with or constantly complaining, it's likely that information will get around the grapevine as well.

Sometimes it's warranted—yes, there are impossible authors—but sometimes it's not. Yet fair or not, it can come back to haunt you. So the best thing to do if you run head on into the disappointments that come with having a corporation package your art is to go out for a long walk, kick the mountain, growl at the lizards or do whatever else you do when you want to let off steam . . . then get on with life.

Is this apsect of the business going to be enough to keep you from writing? I hope not. We all cope with the problems one way or another. And one of the best ways is by reminding ourselves that being a writer is the most fun and exciting thing we can think of.

Good heavens, compared to the heartburn, ulcers and teeth gnashing you would experience if you were an agent, editor or publisher, your job is a piece of cake. Just view those various professionals as the wizards to whom you give pages of text that they take behind their green baize curtains and turn into money for you. Not bad, in the long run.

CHAPTER FOURTEEN

Daydreams and Nightmares

Too often the delirium of having a dream come true is followed by a terrible crash, and authors are no more exempt from such letdowns than anyone else. In fact, given the odds we fight against, our triumphs may be doubly extraordinary, our disasters twice as painful. So, on the theory that if you know the course beforehand, you can plan to make up on the straightaway what you lose on the roundabouts, the following is a collection of cautions, hints and validations.

NOW THAT YOU'RE IN PRINT . . .

Every author dreams of the day when the manuscript sells, the book is published, the story optioned by Hollywood and finally made into a movie, complete with the author's name spelled correctly on the screen. (Well, after all the years of starving, the hours of reading and weeks of research, to say nothing of months of writing, surely we have some dream time coming.)

If or when these dreams come true, they are wonderful, glorious and exciting, but like most other things in life, they come with their own share of Catch-22s. The reality doesn't always live up to the promise, and I don't think I ever met a published author who had any notion of how many hassles she would encounter the first time out.

DON'T QUIT YOUR DAY JOB

Just because your novel's sold doesn't mean your financial troubles are over. I've read that in any one year less than 10 percent of all published authors are able to live entirely on their earnings as writers, and that includes *all* kinds of wordsmiths—journalists, how-to writers, scholars and novelists.

Most hold down other jobs. I know an author of young adult books who turned out four to six books a year while she was president of a small but prestigious college in the South. She decided to become a full-time author when she began making as much money writing as she did running the school.

Or there's a well-known fantasy writer who is a stock broker on Wall Street during the day and conjures up award-winning fiction at night.

Both of these people have learned, either through observation or hard experience, that just because your manuscript sells doesn't mean it will support you. In other words, as they say in theater, "don't quit your day job."

Advances are figured very, very carefully, based largely on the number of books the publisher thinks will sell, how much each book will cost both to produce and ship and what the publisher is willing to spend on advertising. All of these things are taken into account when the publisher offers your agent a bid, and the money for these items is basically ALL THE COMPANY PLANS TO SPEND ON THE BOOK, PERIOD.

So while you're sure that as soon as the reading public discovers your work, the publisher will rush to print up thousands more copies, the publishers figure they'll be happy if they sell the bulk of the first pressrun. Keep in mind, MOST BOOKS DON'T EARN OUT and MOST AUTHORS DON'T SEE ANY EXTRA ROYAL-TIES. That's how good the publishers are at calculating advances.

Even if your work makes it onto the local best-seller list, the publishers may decide not to do the usual follow-up advertising simply because they know they're going to get what they expected out of the deal and see no reason to spend any more. It's their investment, after all, and they'll guard it closely.

Best-Sellers are a slightly different critter, but they're usually decided on BEFORE THE CONTRACT IS EVEN SIGNED. A few books develop legs on their own, but the work that becomes a true best-seller simply by capturing the public's fancy is rare indeed.

Generally it's the agent who starts the whole thing going by informing one or several publishers there's a strong best-seller for sale. If your agent truly believes in it, he will sweep the publishers up in so much enthusiasm, they'll be convinced it's going to earn them tons of money before they even lay eyes on the manuscript. (Obviously agents have to be very *cautious* and very *sure* before

pushing a book at this level, as it only takes a couple of miscalcula-
tions to have publishers begin to question the agents' judgment.)

There are several ways to get a best-seller rolling. One way is for
the agent to go to the publisher directly (no acquisitions editor
here) and offer the manuscript to him over lunch; another is to
put the book up for auction. In either of these events, everyone at
the publisher's knows this is the BIG BOOK OF THE LINE, and
works on it accordingly, giving it first priority and taking pride in
having a hand in it. Indeed, one professional says Best-Seller Fever
can sweep through an entire firm, with editors, art directors, copy-
editors and secretaries all taking the manuscript home to read
overnight or on weekends, then talking it up to their counterparts
in other houses, so when review copies go out to the critics, everyone in the industry is waiting.

These are the books the publishers spend their advertising budgets on; the ones they have parties to launch; the works they set
up authors' tours for. Even before the first books are shipped the
jacket covers proclaim "Best-Seller," so naturally the publishers
are going to try to make that happen.

Occasionally (but far less often), it is the book itself that gets
things going. For instance, when Harper & Row bought Colleen
McCullough's *The Thorn Birds,* they treated it as just another gothic
romance—nothing to write home about, surely. But in those days
(1977) contracts were made with a hardcover house and the paperback rights auctioned off separately. (Because of all the mergers
since then, most big publishers have both hard- and softcover imprints under their umbrellas, and many contracts are for both
editions, with the paperback automatically coming out a year after
the hardcover.)

Anyhow, the paperback houses got so excited about *The Thorn
Birds,* they bid the price right through the roof and suddenly
Harper & Row had to take notice. They managed to turn the manuscript around in almost record time, bringing out the hardcover
three months later, and sold more copies of it than of any other
novel since *Gone With the Wind.* This was a case of the book itself
generating the enthusiasm, though long before the reading public
got their hands on it.

The Bridges of Madison County was a different story. The book was
just another romance as far as the publisher was concerned, with
no advertising or hoopla attached to it. Not only that, it came out

during a major recession when bookstores were having a hard time staying afloat.

As I understand it, one enterprising bookseller put *Bridges* up next to the cash register—it's a small book—and began touting the fact that it only cost $14.95, could be read in an evening, and was a touching story written by a man. His ploy worked well enough to get it out into the reading public, who began to tell their friends about it. The bookseller then told all his friends at the American Booksellers Association convention that the book had paid his rent month after month, and pretty soon everyone was pushing it. That was a case where it was the retailers, not the publisher, who made the book a best-seller.

Some twenty years before, another man had written another small romance that became a massive best-seller (ever wonder about the cyclic nature of such things—maybe every generation needs to discover that men are romantics too?). But *Love Story* was a carefully planned production, as I recall. The tale of the preppy boy falling in love with and marrying the junk dealer's daughter, only to have her die of leukemia, was in fact the true story a graduate student told his professor, who immediately called a cohort at one of the Hollywood studios and said, "Boy, do I have a story for you!" After hearing the tale, the moviemaker suggested it be written up as a book first and pushed as a best-seller so the studio would have an already established audience when the movie came out. No sooner said than done.

So if best-sellers are manufactured by hype and marketing, do they ever fail? Sure they do; you just don't notice it. When you pick up a book you've never heard of with a jacket that proclaims "Best-Seller," you just figure it's your lack of knowledge, right? Well, now you know better.

MAKING THE BEST-SELLER LIST

Say your novel does truly make it onto the local best-seller list. What happens then? First off, you thank your agent or publisher (or both, if they both call to tell you of your new standing), then you go out on the street and do a little dance, a lot of hollering or some quick laps around the track, depending on how you express unbelievable joy and excitement. Great balls of fire, you've got it made! Haven't you? Well, sort of.

The Dynamics of A True Best-Seller show how little input you have in the destiny of your book. At the end of every week regional lists are compiled, based on some sort of publishing alchemy that includes the titles most reordered plus the sales records of certain select and (usually) secret sample stores, and the result is the regional best-seller list. Not only does every publisher watch this closely to see what "units are moving" that week, but all the national chains pay close attention, too.

So it's not uncommon for a store manager in Grand Rapids to say, "Gee, Atlanta sold a bunch of Such and Such last week; maybe we should feature it at the front of the store and see if we can do as well." This way, what begins in one area spreads throughout the country, and eventually the book makes it to the national best-seller lists.

Sometimes other regions will wait to see if the title moves up the list after its initial debut; it might die out if there's no support. If the publisher is going to back your work with advertising, this is when local newspaper ads kick in. (Your agent may nudge the publisher in that direction, but you'd best not or you're likely to be told "stick to writing manuscripts and let us handle the marketing.")

Often the publisher will expect one of the chains to go in on a newspaper ad, and if the store doesn't, you may never see the ad, your book may slip back into oblivion and that's the end of that. Save that week's best-seller list anyway, because even if it's twelfth in a field of twelve, through fluke or talent your book did bask for a moment in its natural glory.

THINGS YOU CAN'T DO ANYTHING ABOUT

As you're no doubt realizing, there is much that is beyond your control where your book is concerned—everything from titles and covers to advertising and marketing. These last two are considered essential in protecting the publisher's investment, and no amount of common sense is going to sway the powers that be, once they make up their minds to do something. Their decisions do, however, make a major difference in what happens to your book after it gets set in type.

Advertising

Forget whatever promises the publishers made beforehand; if it's not written in the contract, they're not likely to do it. This is particularly true if there's a long wait between when you sign the contract and when they bring out your book. Perhaps it's a matter of lost momentum or dissipating enthusiasm, or maybe they forget they said they were going to do a national advertising campaign, with an author's tour and the whole works. That was promised *before* you signed the contract, and times are different now.

Also, you have only your one fledgling to focus on, but your publisher may have twenty or thirty books out at once. And since the company is basing everything on bottom-line economics, if some other book in the line has gotten hot, it will naturally command all the publisher's attention. More than one firm has pulled ALL its budget from every other book in order to boost the one that's suddenly doing well. If it's *your* book they're pushing, well and good. But if it's not, your only consolation may be that you're not the only one forsaken.

Nobody says it's fair, particularly if they told you they would support your work, but you've little recourse other than to grit your teeth and bear it, unless they put their promise of advertising in writing (which would be very rare for a first novel).

Marketing

This is another important area over which you'll have no say, and for which you need to depend on your editor. Sometimes, however, even she can't do much for you because the publisher will market your book based on what he thinks will sell, not what you actually wrote.

For instance, if you're a euhemerist retelling a myth from a realistic, historical point of view, and your agent encouraged you to sign with a publisher who, unbeknownst to you, wants to break into the fantasy field, you may find your book being marketed in the science fiction/fantasy department of the bookstores even though you wrote for a mainstream audience and there's *no fantasy* in it at all.

Or consider the case of the author who spent years researching unusual women of Regency England, two of whom she wrote about in different books. The publisher brought them out as women's romance (which is *not* what she wrote), and while the first one did well enough in sales, the second didn't hit the sixty thousand "units sold" that the publisher took as the minimum sale acceptable for romance, so the author was dropped.

There's a further problem with this kind of mismarketing in that it has a ripple effect; books put out as genre (fantasy, women's or historical romance, mysteries and westerns) are generally only advertised in and reviewed by genre magazines for fans who, predictably enough, find novels about real people a paltry substitute for the fantasy, romance or western they prefer. Also, many newspapers don't even bother to review genre books, so you may get short shrift there as well.

Add to this the fact that genre books are usually kept in a separate section in the bookstore under fantasy, romance or western. Mainstream readers rarely prowl through these sections to see if anything they might enjoy has been misidentified. Thus much of the audience you wrote for may never even hear of your book, or if they hear of it, they don't find it on the fiction shelves and so leave, disappointed.

While there is nothing you as the author can do about this problem of trying to reach your readership, it does underline once again why it is important to find an agent who understands what you write and will offer it to a publisher who will target the same market you wrote for. It's also important that you realize if you're writing mainstream, historical fiction, not "genre" with it's built-in marketing slots, the chances of your getting any real money as an advance are limited. This is not because your agent isn't doing his job, but because most publishers don't see how to make money with it.

Reviews

These are the bane and delight of most authors; some critics are going to love your work while others hate it. There are always going to be some who carp about one thing or another. *Kirkus Reviews* is one of the major publications used by libraries and bookstores to decide what to buy. If Kirkus pans your efforts, consider it an initiation rite into the league of published authors.

Library Journal is directed specifically at libraries and is known for its fairness and thorough approach to new books. Reviewers concentrate on reviewing the work and not on criticism.

Publishers Weekly is the industry's standard and is conscientious about reviewing new works. Sybil Steinberg, who handles the review section of the magazine, suggests that authors gently remind their editors about sending *PW* a review copy SIX WEEKS before the book comes out so the reviewer has time to read it and do a review before the actual publication date. (The PUB DATE is your book's official birthday, after which all the hoopla stops while everyone moves on to the next book or line. Your work will be in the stores *weeks* before that, and most promotion—as well as advertising—takes place before the pub date. Therefore reviewers need to have access to your work before then.)

Naturally you'll be aware of any local reviews and should alert friends, family and anyone else you know at a distance who might run into reviews of your work to pass them along. One author got a review from a fan who saw someone else reading it in a newspaper on an airplane. When the travelers deplaned, the fan grabbed the paper and sent the review page to the author. Although your agent and publisher will usually have clipping services on the lookout for mention of your work, things often slip through the cracks, so try to keep an eye out yourself.

If you're like most authors, you'll discover one reviewer somewhere in this country who both sees and understands more clearly than anyone else what you were trying to do in your book. There is always a temptation to contact such a reviewer with a personal note, though it may be overstepping the lines of professionalism. I simply wrote to mine and told her how much I appreciated both her perception and her thoroughness, and if she ever turned around and said, "Woolley missed the mark on this one," I'd take another hard look at where I'd gone wrong.

As far as unpleasant or unflattering reviews, forget them. While it might be tempting to point out that the reviewers are criticizing oranges when you wrote about apples, it won't do any good. Mostly just be grateful for whatever coverage you get and let it go at that. And yes, do keep copies of the reviews, even the bad ones (you don't have to go back and reread them just because they're in your folder). You never know when being able to send a copy of a review, complete with date and name of both the publication and reviewer, will come in handy.

Royalty Statements

I'm including these in the section on things you can't do anything about because it is virtually impossible to hurry them and often difficult to make sense of what they purport to tell you.

To begin with, most contracts specify that the publisher will provide the author with a statement twice a year, for the six months from, say, March to September. The statement will note how many books were ordered by bookstores during this time, and you will be credited for those sales. However, the publishers used to argue— perhaps with some merit—that it took time to count inventories, compile paperwork and so forth, so they gave themselves up to three months *after* the sales period ended in which to give you an accounting, during which time they were sitting on whatever money they owed you and pocketing the interest it earned.

Nowadays the warehouse inventory is all on computers, and with a touch of a button your editor can pull up the current figures on how many books were printed, how many remain in the warehouse and what happened to *most* of the rest of them. So it's ludicrous for publishers to claim it takes months to determine how many you sold and how much to put against your advance. Some still take three months to pay, however, either out of respect for a sacred tradition or for more mercenary reasons.

More importantly, what has been shipped to the bookstores and what you get credited with are generally two different amounts. That's because it's assumed that a certain number of your books will be returned by the bookstores, so the publisher holds back a percentage of what you've earned in what is called "reserve against returns." Reserves can range anywhere from 5 to 40 percent; in the last case, for instance, you're only credited with 60 percent of the monies you've earned.

This practice of holding money against returns generally comes as a shock to the new author. While the concept is defensible— bookstores traditionally have the right to return unsold or damaged volumes—how the pubulishers arrive at the percentage they expect to be returned and whether that figure proves to be accurate or not too often get lost in the shuffle. Some publishers adjust the amount later when they have an actual book count to go on, while others seem to just let it ride with the estimate.

In a March 16, 1992 article called "Cooking the Books," *Forbes* magazine reports that any publisher who wants to cheat finds the vagueness of reserves a handy place to do so; it's an area that's hard to pin down and easy to defend.

Not all publishers cheat their authors, by any matter of means, and mistakes can happen. But many authors, confronted with conflicting sales numbers from their editors and their statements, begin to grow suspicious and think about exercising their rights to an audit.

Audits

Most contracts promise you can examine the publisher's books at any time; it's fairly standard policy. One would think that such scrutiny would prevent the publisher from indulging in creative bookeeping, but audits are very expensive and can take months to accomplish. Added to that is the fact that most standard contracts say if the publisher is within 5 to 10 percent of being honest, *you* have to pay for the audit. As Kirsch notes in his *Kirsch's Handbook of Publishing Law*, this is designed both to discourage audits and to shift the cost to the author, which explains why only big-name novelists resort to them. (The Forbes article reported an audit initiated by such an author. When it developed his publisher owed him $500,000 more than had been reported over the years, the company seems to have paid up immediately.)

Sometimes, if there's a flagrant breach of contract, the Writers' Union or Authors' Guild have funded an author's audit, in order to make an example of the offending publisher. But for the most part new authors have to swallow their suspicions and simply hope for the best.

Many authors end up angry and disillusioned with their publishers, what with having no control over marketing or advertising and seeming to be totally at the mercy of them financially. Yes, that's the downside of being a published novelist. But there are many other wonderful upsides, which I'll get to as soon as we talk about what you can do to make sure you're in a more powerful position where the finances are concerned.

Learn To Read Your Statements

As confusing as they are, it's worth it to pay attention to what your publisher is reporting. About five years ago the bigger houses were in the habit of sending out multipage statements so convoluted that one publisher actually sent its authors a book on how to read them. I'm told some larger houses are going to simpler statements now, however.

There are several ways to keep abreast of your statements. First off is simple mathematics: ALWAYS CHECK THE ARITHMETIC, both in numbers sold and in the calculation of what your percentage should be, because sometimes arithmetical mistakes show up. (This is just sound advice for every bill or statement of any kind. People can, quite innocently, punch in the wrong numbers.)

Secondly, check to make sure the publisher is adhering to the contracted royalty schedule. Some publishers sign a new novelist at a certain schedule, then *just before* the book goes to press suddenly announce, "Gee whiz, we can't afford to give you that fast an increase on royalties, so we're cutting it down to so-and-so." Eager to get into print, first time authors end up agreeing whether they want to nor not.

This is not a new practice, and as much as one argues that contracts are contracts and authors can't make unilateral changes in their own favor, as far as I can determine there's nothing you can do to stop it, unless your contract specifically forbids it or agents refuse to ask their authors to go along with it.

Sometimes, if the publisher has arm-wrestled the author to the mat on this one, the royalty department may take it's pick of whichever schedule pays out the least money, depending on how big or little the sales are. *That's* something you can redress by being sure they adhere to the most recently agreed-upon rate of increase.

Most agents try to go over the statements they receive for their clients; as with advances, the statements come to the agent and are then sent on to the author. But agents are busy finding out who wants what, or looking at new manuscripts and tying down already negotiated contracts, so sometimes things hidden inside an old contract slip by. As my agent told me, "Yes, we keep an eye on the statements, but you, as the concerned author, should check them even more closely, just to be on the safe side."

Naturally if you find a discrepancy in the royalty schedule or the rate, the number of books sold, lost or still in the warehouse as compared to the number in the pressrun, or in simple arithmetic, contact your agent. If you've made a mistake, the agent should hasten to explain it so you no longer feel cheated. If it's the publisher who's mistaken, a good agent will see that the author is compensated as soon as possible, without any shilly-shallying.

WHAT HAPPENED TO THE UPSIDE?

In spite of the vicissitudes just outlined, there are still many wonderful aspects to being an author, over and above the fact that you obviously love writing or you wouldn't have gotten this far with your project.

First off, the very fact that your book got published says some people in the industry recognized your talent, energy and perseverance. They believed in your storytelling ability enough to invest thousands of dollars to get it before the public, and they probably included a clause in the contract that says they have the right of first refusal on your next novel as well.

Secondly, now that you're a published novelist, you have a chance to develop a following. Most of us have to build up our audience one book at a time, and you've just taken the first steps toward that. And there are few things more surprising (or wonderful) than having a stranger suddenly recognize your name and ask, "Did you write that book I just finished—and loved?" It does happen and no lack or presence of hype can equal the pleasure of unsolicited praise from an unknown fan.

Fans are the people who keep us all in business, so be very, very nice to them. When you do signings, whether at a local bookstore or out on an author's tour, give each reader your full attention when it's her turn—I've seen both Colleen McCullough and Morgan Llewelyn (who wrote *Bard, Horse Goddess* and *The Lion of Ireland*) signing books when they were so tired they could drop, still being incredibly gracious. It's part of being a pro.

If fans write to you, answer as soon as you can. If such mail was sent via the publisher, it may be delayed for weeks or months, so answering immediately is important. Some authors limit their correspondence to fancy postcards, which allows for a handwritten "thank-you" note returned in a timely fashion but precludes any temptation to spend lots of time writing whole letters.

Awards, such as the Pulitzer, National Book Award, etc., have varying rules as to how they arrive at recipients. The *LMP* has a section on awards, and there are many, from internationally known to totally obscure, so take the time to go over them; there may be some you and your book will qualify for.

If you can't submit your book for consideration, both your agent and your editor should know that you're interested. Some authors are, others aren't; some publishers care, some don't; and some books are more suitable for such things than others. Ask your professionals what the chances are, and abide (peacefully) by their decisions; they know this business better than you do.

Promotion through the publisher is a double-edged sword. Only best-selling authors are sent on tour from one city to another, which seems a little ludicrous since the public already knows about them. However, it does make for more book sales, so everyone benefits. But authors' tours are incredibly tiring, and you're likely to find you're booked into three different cities in one day, if the publisher can arrange it. Because of the costs involved, authors' tours are becoming more and more passé, however. Which brings us to what you can do to further your own public relations.

BLOWING YOUR OWN HORN

John Kremer, who specializes in showing people how to get attention, has written *1001 Ways to Market Your Books For Authors and Publishers*. Beginning with the basics of marketing, he then goes into everything from how to get speaking engagements, interviews and signings, to a special section on writing press releases and bios.

Moreover, there are many simple things you can take care of as soon as the book is in print. First off, make sure all local newspapers and television stations know you (1) live in the area; (2) have a new book out; and (3) are available to be interviewed. Be prepared to send them a bio and a review copy of your book, plus anything that points out the relevance of your work for their audiences. They'll go over most of this information before deciding whether to have you on the air or not, and since you're local, they may even read the book first.

TV and Press interviews are a lot less likely to happen for a novelist than for the author of a nonfiction work. You may consider this a blessing since interviewers outside your own area are much less likely to have read your book. The result is inane questions and blank reactions. (When I was a journalist, the actors, authors and musicians I spoke with were often shocked that I'd actually seen, read or listened to their works; they were so used to being interviewed by people who hadn't done their homework.) This situation is almost endemic on the larger TV morning talk programs, where the person on the screen just asks the questions the producer gives him, without having any idea what the book's all about. If you got on such a show, enjoy the novelty of it, but don't feel you've missed much if it doesn't turn out that way.

Book Signings are a natural for you to arrange with your local bookstores, even if the publisher won't help with posters, book covers, fliers or newspaper ads. Chances are the local papers will be writing you up on the human interest level if not the literary pages, and if they can note that you'll be signing your books at such and such a store, they'll be delivering news to their readers as well. Since the bookstore will be getting a free plug, most everyone wins.

Notify the Libraries, Museums, Historical Societies (and other such groups that you used as resources) when the book comes out. If you can get the publisher to send them complimentary copies, so much the better, because publishers only provide authors with the number of free volumes agreed to in the contract. Sometimes you can order more (to be charged against your royalties) or see if your local bookstore will order a bunch for you, then pay them the wholesale price. It's always a good idea to have a stash of books on hand, just in case.

Many of the groups you met while doing your research will be delighted to have you make a personal appearance, along with a stack of books that you or they can sell. This is a nice way to thank the people who were helpful to you and let them make some extra money through the book sales as well. (Always coordinate this sort of thing with the local bookstore managers, however, to see if they want to handle the selling of books at the event. You must never undercut the retail stores, either in actual price or in opportunity to sell, as they are your basic pipeline to the public.)

Check Out the Bookstores wherever you go to see if they have copies of your book, and if so, offer to sign them. Many stores, big and little, put autographed copies on special display, as it helps with sales.

Get Business Cards Made Up with your name and the title of your book so that when you are talking to people who say they'd be interested in reading it, you can hand them a card with all the pertinent information and not have to go rummaging about for paper and pencil. I know several romance authors who have the book's title, publisher, pub date, ISBN number (for ordering) and price all printed up on postcards that they then send off to everyone on their mailing lists. This is an expense you simply need to decide about on your own; it is not likely to be picked up by your publisher, but can come off your taxes as a business expense.

Schools, Book Clubs and Writers Groups are always looking for people to augment their curriculum or programs, and if you enjoy that sort of thing, by all means let them know you're willing and available. Some authors like that kind of contact, while others hate it, so it's pretty much your call.

These are all the sorts of things you can do in your hometown, but what happens if your book stirs up enough interest that it actually makes it to Hollywood? Grab your hat in one hand and the fringe of the flying carpet in the other because it's bound to be a roller-coaster ride!

IT SHOULD ONLY HAPPEN

The number of books that are optioned by Hollywood compared to the number that get published every year is small indeed. And out of the optioned properties, only one in ten actually gets turned into a theater film, TV movie or video release. So the chances are slim. Still, it does happen.

Hollywood Agents are a breed apart—some very smooth and slick, some truly honest and professional. But there are a lot who are pushy, gushy and so full of the typical L.A. hype, even a rube from the sticks can spot it. Therefore it's usually best to let your literary agent handle the whole deal. Even if they agree to split their fees, you'll end up paying both agents something, and it's probably well worth missing the aggravation, high-pressure tactics and innumerable headaches to let your literary agent handle it all. (This is where belonging to a large agency helps, as the large agencies often have Hollywood specialists who can handle these deals for you.) Still and all, it helps to know what to watch for.

The Hollywood Hype includes praising your work (or the "concept" if the agent hasn't actually read it). She'll tell you how well it will translate to the screen, who all she envisions in the production—Julia Roberts, Tom Cruise, Bruce Willis; the names trip off her tongue even as she throws around references to the great credits the producer has behind him. (Don't hesitate to write these credits down and call the Motion Picture Academy or the National Academy of Television Arts and Sciences, where you can ask to confirm whether that producer really did make that specific movie or miniseries or won the awards the agent claims. There's also the Producers' Guild, which will tell you if he is a member in good standing. After all, you have a right to know the honesty of the person you're talking business with, and while the producer may be all everyone says he is, it's amazing how Hollywood types are willing to say anything to close the deal.)

There will be much assurance that you'll love the result, it will be honest to the historical era, locale, character portrayal, etc. All they want is that you not let anyone else purchase the rights to make the film until they've had a chance to line up money, script, actors and production crew. They will pay you for this; it's known as an option and may be seen as a kind of down payment, which is usually deducted from the agreed-upon final price if they do go ahead and make the film.

Options can be for various time periods, from several months to a year or more. When the time on the option runs out, it gets renewed or renegotiated or it lapses. There are some books that have been under option for more than a decade; they keep being renewed or renegotiated but never get made into film. The author, however, gets the option payment every year, which doesn't hurt. (I've been told there are some writers who live fairly comfortably on such infusions, without having to do another book.) However, IF AND WHEN THE PRODUCER COMES UP WITH THE MONEY TO MAKE THE FILM, YOU ARE BOUND BY WHATEVER THE OPTION AGREEMENT CONTAINED.

Actual Production cannot legally start without the full payment of the agreed-upon price, but you may never see ANY further form of paperwork; everything will have been covered by the option papers. So you need to understand and be satisfied with that, including the fact that you are signing away ALL film rights to your story FOREVER. Even if they make a product that has *nothing* to do with what you wrote, you will never have a chance to see it remade in a more faithful rendition. IF THAT IS OF CONCERN TO YOU, READ ON.

There are a hundred ways that Hollywood has found to slicker the unwary, and these methods work even on some who should have known better.

One way to weasel around an author is to negotiate for one kind of production—say a four-hour television miniseries for *x* amount of money—but when the option papers arrive they say a *minimum* of two hours for half the amount.

If the author refuses to accept the lower time and amount, the agent and/or producer can affect enormous outrage, claim that the deal was struck verbally and threaten to sue the author for breach of contract. Indeed, if you did say, "Yes, your company can have it," you've essentially sealed its fate, for in California a verbal agreement is as binding as a written one, and when it comes to the amount, that's just your word against the producer's. It's known as playing hardball, and the many agents and producers are very good at it.

All of which leads to the following simple pieces of advice:

1. *Never* **Agree to Anything Verbally.** This is the first commandment, and should be graven on the inside of your eyelids. No matter what an agent, actor, producer, director or production company is proposing, you smile pleasantly, allow as how it sounds fascinating, and ask them to "please put it in writing so my agent and I can consider it."

2. Never Talk to the People Who Want to Buy Your Property Alone. Always make sure your agent is either in on the conference call or relaying messages between you and the potential buyer. Keep your agent in the middle, and record in notes everything you discuss with him and the buyer. Just be sure not to agree to anything until you've had a chance to see it in writing.

3. Remember That Nothing Is Set In A Contract *Until* You've Agreed To It, But Once You Do Agree To It, You Have To Live With It. This holds for every sentence and clause, and anyone, even your own agent, who tells you something is "just standard boilerplate and doesn't mean anything" may be trying to put something over on you. Legally everything is up for negotiation, so make your agent or the buyer explain anything you don't understand or agree with.

4. Always Assume That The Buyer Will Go With Whatever The Minimum Is In Writing, No Matter What They Say In Person. (You've probably already learned this from your publishing contracts.)

5. When They Are Ready To Put Their Offer In Writing, Have Them Send A Copy To Your Attorney As Well.

What? Pay an attorney hundreds per hour when the darn agents are already going to be getting their cuts as well? *You bet,* as long as the attorney specializes in literary and film contracts and knows all the things to watch for. She is the only one without a vested interest in the sale and will therefore represent *you* fairly and honorably.

There are lots of other little tricks to keep an eye out for, such as the producer promising that the author will receive another chunk of money for each million dollar increase in the film's budget. Sounds simple and straightforward—as the production becomes bigger and more lavish, you get a larger amount for it. But have you ever noticed how many movies are made by production companies you've never heard of? These unknown firms come into existence purely for the life of the production, and by the time you've found out that they've shot the film and you make your request for a financial accounting, they will have paid off those they choose to and gone out of business—poof, disappeared, no longer around to be held accountable.

Not only will they not necessarily let you know when it's being shot, you might not even know when it's going to be released or shown on TV, unless you know someone in the industry. Your attorney will probably be able to get that information for you, and with luck you can talk with the PR people at the TV network office if it's on the tube.

Remember, the network people didn't try to cheat you out of anything, and honey catches more advance tape copies than vinegar. Make friends with whomever you can so you'll have some forewarning both on the quality of the film and when it will be aired. (They'll always tell you it's great, even if they haven't seen it, so don't take their word; just thank them profusely for sending on a viewing tape.)

What If It Turns Out To Be A Dog? Best I can say is put in a supply of dog biscuits and Kleenex. If it's truly awful, you'll probably end up crying for the actors as well as your story.

Some authors refuse to even see their works adapted for the screen, while others gird up their courage and sneak off to some quiet spot to view it incognito—when you're home alone, if it's on tape, or in an obscure neighborhood theater, if it's a big-screen release. If it gets too bad you can always walk out, or turn it off, after all.

Has Hollywood ever done a *good* adaptation of a historical novel? Well, you can't get much better than *Gone With the Wind* for being true to the book, but Mitchell's contract pretty well tied the producer's hands, since she had approval of practically everything having to do with the script. The result was about the closest possible translation from one medium to another. (If you have a massive best-seller, you're more likely to retain creative control or right of approval over the script, or get yourself included on the staff as a "consultant," though I have a hunch that might be more woe than wonderful.) Still, *Gone With the Wind* was the rarity.

Even though David Lean did a remarkable job with *Doctor Zhivago*, if you compare the film to the book, you'll find the feel of it is considerably different. The movie is much more lush and romantic, like a Russian *Gone With the Wind*, and it elides entirely the last portion of the book.

Not that I'm knocking it; it's splendid screen fare, and far more historically accurate than most films. When a PR person from the TV network mentioned that my Guinevere was being shot in Lithuania, my jaw dropped in amazement as I asked why.

"Oh, the castles are prettier there," he said.

"But my people lived in mud huts and Roman ruins . . ." I sputtered.

"Not any more."

So What Do You Do? Hollywood is not the only place where you'll run into a patch of nettles when you thought you were headed for a bed of roses as an author. (There's the signing at the store where the books have not arrived, or equally disastrous, there are stacks of books, and no one comes. As Parke Godwin quipped, you can always spot the author because he's sitting there by himself, "lonely as a seagull on a piling." If you're ever faced with this, it helps to know we've all been there at least once

Someday you'll look back and laugh about the time you were interviewed on live TV by a host who thought your family saga, called *Blood Ties*, was a true-life suspense thriller about a mass murderer. You name it, if you're a published novelist, you'll probably run into it!

Yet Hollywood seems a fitting end to this overview of the good, the bad and the ludicrous aspects of being a historical novelist. It's all done with smoke and mirrors, and as many authors advise, take the money and run. Just make sure it's a big enough chunk that you won't regret losing those rights forever.

On the more serious side, there's always the consolation of having gotten farther with this book than you ever thought possible. After all, how many other authors do you know who had even a Hollywood dog made out of their work?

So the best I can say is don't cry, sweetie, you'll know better next time.

IS IT ALL WORTH IT?

Good heavens, what a question!

I firmly believe that writers write because we write. There is something in us that wants to capture it all on paper, and whether anyone else ever sees it or not isn't nearly as important as flinging out that net of words.

I do make a distinction between writers and authors, with the latter being those who try to make a living at it. It's bound to toughen, if not harden, us, and I don't blame anyone who completes a manuscript and then decides to put it into a bureau drawer and go on with his next project.

But whether that project is another book or simply the rest of your life, you'll have had the thrill of writing your very own novel, of playing with history and people and learning more about your chosen era than you ever would have otherwise.

If, on the other hand, you do decide to risk the publishing waters, my best goes with you, and I hope this book will prove useful in keeping you afloat if the waters get choppy. At the very least you'll know you're not crazy, you're just another author trying to stay sane in a crazy business.

INDEX

More Great Books for Writers!

The Writer's Guide to Everyday Life From Prohibition Through World War II—Uncover all the details you need to add color, depth and a ring-of-truth to your work. You'll find an intimate look at what life was like back then, including popular slang, the Prohibition, the Depression, World War II, crime, transportation, fashion, radio, music and much more! *#10450/$18.99/272 pages*

The Writer's Guide to Everyday Life in Renaissance England—Fill your work with the day-to-day details that make writing authentic! This lively, authoritative reference is the only one of its kind—a new view of Renaissance England, brimming with the details of daily life—from fashions and table customs to religion and courtship. With this volume at your side, you'll have everything you need to paint an authentic picture of the time! *#10484/$18.99/272 pages/20 b&w illus.*

The Writer's Guide to Everyday Life in the Middle Ages—This time-travel companion will guide you through the medieval world of Northwestern Europe. Discover the facts on dining habits, clothing, armor, festivals, religious orders and much more—everything you need to paint an authentic picture. *#10423/$17.99/256 pages*

The Writer's Guide to Everyday Life in the 1800's—From clothes to food, social customs to furnishings, you'll find everything you need to write an accurate story about this century. Plus, the entries are dated so you don't invent something before its creation. *#10353/$18.99/320 pages*

The Writer's Guide to Everyday Life in Colonial America—Paint a true picture of what life was like in the American colonies. You'll find details on food and drink, clothing, architecture, religion, trade and important events from 1598-1783. *#10504/$18.99/288 pages*

1997 Writer's Market: Where & How to Sell What You Write—Get your work into the right buyers' hands and save yourself the frustration of getting manuscripts returned in the mail. You'll find 4,000 listings loaded with submission information, as well as real life interviews on scriptwriting, networking, freelancing and more! *#10457/$27.99/1008 pages*

Now Available on CD-ROM!

1997 Writer's Market Electronic Edition—Customize your marketing research and speed to the listings that fit your needs using this compact, searchable CD-ROM! *#10520/$39.99*

1997 Writer's Market Combination Package—For maximum usability, order both the book and CD-ROM in one convenient package! *#45148/$49.99*

1997 Novel & Short Story Writer's Market—Get the information you need to get your short stories and novels published. You'll discover 1,900 listed fiction publishers in this new edition, plus original articles on fiction writing techniques; detailed subject categories to help you target appropriate publishers; and interviews with writers, publishers and editors! *#10493/$22.99/672 pages*

The Writer's Essential Desk Reference—Get quick, complete, accurate answers to your important writing questions with this companion volume to *Writer's Market*. You'll cover all aspects of the business side of writing—from information on the World Wide Web and other research sites to opportunities with writer's workshops and the basics on taxes and health insurance. *#10485/$24.99/384 pages*

Writing and Selling Your Novel—Weave the facts and philosophy of fiction to write novels that editors and readers are begging to read. In this completely revised edition, you'll master the art of writing publishable fiction from start to finish as you learn to develop effective work habits, refine your fiction technique and tailor your novels for tightly targeted markets. *#10509/$17.99/208 pages*

Discovering the Writer Within: 40 Days to More Imaginative Writing—Uncover the creative individual inside who will, with encouragement, turn secret thoughts and special moments into enduring words. You'll learn how to find something exciting in unremarkable places, write punchy first sentences for imaginary stories, give a voice to inanimate objects and much more! *#10472/$14.99/192 pages/paperback*

The Writer's Digest Sourcebook for Building Believable Characters—Create unforgettable characters as you "attend" a roundtable where six novelists reveal their approaches to characterization. You'll probe your characters' backgrounds, beliefs and desires with a fill-in-the-blanks questionnaire. And a thesaurus of characteristics will help you develop the many other features no character should be without. *#10463/$17.99/288 pages*

The Writer's Legal Guide, Revised Edition—Now the answer to all your legal questions is right at your fingertips! The updated version of this treasured desktop companion contains essential information on business issues, copyright protection and registration, contract negotiation, income taxation, electronic rights and much, much more. *#10478/$19.95/256 pages/paperback*

How to Write Attention-Grabbing Query & Cover Letters—Use the secrets Wood reveals to write queries perfectly tailored, too good to turn down! In this guidebook, you will discover why boldness beats blandness in queries every time, ten basics you *must* have in your article queries, ten query blunders that can destroy publication chances and much more. *#10462/$17.99/208 pages*

Writing to Sell—You'll discover high-quality writing and marketing counsel in this classic writing guide from well-known agent Scott Meredith. His timeless advice will guide you along the professional writing path as you get help with creating characters, plotting a novel, placing your work, formatting a manuscript, deciphering a publishing contract—even combating a slump! *#10476/$17.99/240 pages*

The Writer's Ultimate Research Guide—Save research time and frustration with the help of this guide. 352 information-packed pages will point you straight to the information you need to create better, more accurate fiction and nonfiction. *#10447/$19.99/336 pages*

Characters & Viewpoint—Discover how to make your work come alive with vivid, credible, true-to-life characters. Card shows you how to choose the best vantage point for your reader to see the events of your short story or novel unfold. *#10067/$15.99/192 pages*

How to Write Like an Expert About Anything—Find out how to use new technology and traditional research methods to get the information you need; envision new markets and write proposals that sell; find and interview experts on any topic and much more! *#10449/$17.99/224 pages*

Setting—Don't ignore setting as a key to powerful, moving fiction. Jack Bickham, author of over 80 published novels, demonstrates how to use sensual detail and vivid language to paint the perfect setting for your story. *#10397/$14.99/176 pages*

The Writer's Digest Guide to Good Writing—In one book, you'll find the best in writing instruction gleaned from the past 75 years of *Writer's Digest* magazine! Successful authors like Vonnegut, Steinbeck, Oates, Michener and over a dozen others share their secrets on writing technique, idea generation, inspiration and getting published. *#10391/$18.99/352 pages*

Writing for Money—Discover where to look for writing opportunities—and how to make them pay off. You'll learn how to write for magazines, newspapers, radio and TV, newsletters, greeting cards and a dozen other hungry markets! *#10425/$17.99/256 pages*

The Writer's Digest Character Naming Sourcebook—Forget the guesswork! 20,000 first and last names (and their meanings!) from around the world will help you pick the perfect name to reflect your character's role, place in history and ethnicity. *#10390/$18.99/352 pages*

Write Tight—Discover how to say exactly what you want with grace and power, using the right word and the right number of words. Specific instruction and helpful exercises will help you make your writing compact, concise and precise. *#10360/$16.99/192 pages*

Fiction Writer's Workshop—Explore each aspect of the art of fiction including point of view, description, revision, voice and more. At the end of each chapter you'll find more than a dozen writing exercises to help you put what you've learned into action. *#48003/$17.99/256 pages*

Revision: A Creative Approach to Writing and Rewriting Fiction—Kaplan traces the revision process through every stage of story-writing—providing strategies and criteria to help you pinpoint and fix problems in your work. Kaplan offers a rare and very personal

look at revision by showing how three of his own short stories evolved.
#48024/$18.99/240 pages

Elements of the Writing Craft—This collection of 150 lessons reveals how noted writers have "built" their fiction and nonfiction. Each lesson contains a short passage of work from a distinguished writer, a writer's-eye analysis of the passage, and innovative writing exercises to help you apply the techniques of the masters in your own work. *#48027/$19.99/272 pages*

National Writer's Union Guide to Freelance Rates & Standard Practice—A must-have for all freelancers! Tables and charts compiled from surveys of freelance writers, editors and agents give you the going rates for six major freelance markets. Plus, information on rights, the electronic future and more! *#10440/$19.95/200 pages/paperback*

Get That Novel Started! (And Keep It Going 'Til You Finish)—If you're ready for a no excuses approach to starting and completing your novel, then you're ready for this get-it-going game plan. You'll discover wisdom, experience and advice that helps you latch on to an idea and see it through, while avoiding common writing pitfalls. *#10332/$17.99/176 pages*

The 29 Most Common Writing Mistakes And How to Avoid Them—Weak comparisons, too many adjectives, excessive self-expression—with clarity and good humor, Delton shows how to correct these and 26 other common writing mistakes to help you get published! *#10221/$10.99/96 pages/paperback*

Writing the Short Story: A Hands-On Writing Program—With Jack Bickham's unique "workshop on paper" you'll plan, organize, write, revise and polish a short story. Clear instruction, helpful charts and practical exercises will lead you every step of the way! *#10421/$16.99/224 pages*

Creating Characters: How to Build Story People—Grab the empathy of your reader with characters so real they'll jump off the page. You'll discover how to make characters come alive with vibrant emotion, quirky personality traits, inspiring heroism, tragic weaknesses and other uniquely human qualities. *#10417/$14.99/192 pages/paperback*

Description—Discover how to use detailed description to awaken the reader's senses; advance the story using only relevant description; create original word depictions of people, animals, places, weather and much more! *#10451/$15.99/176 pages*